What's a Golfer to Do?

What's a Golfer to Do?

RON KASPRISKE

and the Editors of *Golf Digest*

ARTISAN

Published by Artisan
A Division of Workman Publishing Company, Inc.
225 Varick Street
New York, NY 10014-4381
www.artisanbooks.com

Library of Congress Cataloging-in-Publication Data

ISBN-13: 978-1-57965-373-6

Design by Stephanie Huntwork

Printed in China
First printing, April 2009

10 9 8 7 6 5 4 3 2 1

Contents

Foreword

The operative word in the title of this book is "golfer." Among sportsmen, it's the highest calling. Not everybody who keeps a set of clubs in the garage is a golfer. Certainly not everybody who shows up once a year in a charity outing qualifies. Not even all those 29 million Americans that the National Golf Foundation calls golfers are, in fact, the real thing.

There are sixty definitions in *The Rules of Golf*, but none defines a golfer. Golfers are more than the sum of their fourteen clubs. It matters not whether you have a handicap or even a golf swing. You don't have to belong to a private club or pass a height or gender or age test. Tiger Woods was a full-fledged golfer at three years old, when he appeared with Bob Hope and Jimmy Stewart on national television.

The first step to being a golfer is to respect the game. You don't move or talk or rip your Velcro when another golfer is swinging. You don't walk in somebody else's area of play, that imaginary chalk line between a golfer's ball and the hole. You know the difference between Robert Trent Jones and Bobby Jones, between Pete Dye and Joe Dey. And you go by the oldest dictum of golf friendship: what's said on the course stays on the course.

Golfers play by the rules. Hitting a lunch ball off the first tee—so long as it's an accepted practice among your foursome—isn't breaking the law. Agreeing to play a "leaf rule" in the fall—that is, allowing a lost ball to be replaced in the vicinity of its disappearance—is totally in bounds. Rounding up your handicap a stroke when you haven't played all winter isn't cheating. And using "the circle of friendship"—an expanding and contracting putter length depending on the state of the match and the generosity of the prevailing winds—is a perfectly fine way to determine which putts will be conceded.

A golfer knows how to do all that stuff, but he or she also knows that you don't tee off in front of the markers, move a ball from behind a tree, ground your club in a hazard, or lie about your score. When you play by yourself and there's no one else around, golfers still play by these rules.

Another thing that defines a golfer is that he or she tries on every shot. Even in practice, Jack Nicklaus carefully aimed the clubface, picked his intermediate target, made painstaking swing preparations, and gave every ball his all-out effort. One of my favorite lines about Ben Hogan is that every shot he hit was 95 percent over by the time the club started away from the ball.

Golfers get mad, but they don't throw clubs. Golfers like to have a little something on the line—is there any better symbol of manhood than relieving your buddy of a couple of bucks? Golfers play quickly and know when to pick it up. Golfers will take a caddie when the opportunity arises. Golfers opt to walk rather than ride in a cart when physically able. Golfers are not deterred by cold and rain, and the only thing better than 18 is 36.

Golfers remove their hat when they go indoors and when they eat, even if it's just a hot dog. I'd like to add that golfers own a sport coat and know where it should be worn. When they get to play at a nice place, golfers don't wear blue jeans either. On those last two points, I'm a bit old-fashioned and prefer collars on my golf shirts too, because the golfers I know look more like Tony Soprano than Tiger Woods in a mock turtleneck.

And if all else fails, you know you can tell a golfer at the end of a round, on the 18th green, when the last putt is holed, because a golfer removes the hat and extends his or her hand to thank each fellow competitor for an enjoyable day. For every golfer knows that even a bad day on the course is better than a good day doing almost anything else.

JERRY TARDE
Editor-in-Chief, *Golf Digest*

Introduction

I still vividly remember my first full round of golf on a regulation course. It was at Orangebrook Golf & Country Club in Hollywood, Florida. I skipped my afternoon classes one day during my junior year in high school to play. It was during this five-and-a-half-hour marathon of bad golf that I encountered no less than a dozen situations in which I was completely baffled as to what to do. I had just recently become interested in the game after watching Jack Nicklaus win the 1986 Masters. I understood birdies and bogeys and the basics of golf, but little else. For instance:

When it was my turn to tee off, did I have to tee the ball behind the markers or just near them? When I hit the ball in the water, could I just drop another ball by the pond, and was it a one-stroke penalty or two? When we reached the green, why did that person give me a dirty look when I walked in front of him? And why was every shot I hit curving to the right?

It seemed like there was this secret code of unwritten rules, guidelines, and etiquette that everyone knew but me. I was petrified of doing anything on the golf course that I didn't see someone else do first. Heck, just learning how to get the ball airborne was hard enough, but now I was being bombarded with all sorts of information that made my head swell. And this round was taking forever!

By the time I reached the final hole, with the sobering thought that my score was north of 120, I wondered why anyone would want to play this game—too hard, too slow, too expensive, and too many rules. But then something amazing happened. After hitting a couple of crappy but manageable shots on the par-5 eighteenth on the East Course, I was about 180 yards from the green. I grabbed this tiny-headed, Patty Berg–model Wilson 3-iron and swung as hard as I could. By some miracle, the right combination of bad swing mechanics and body compensations made the ball jump off the face and track, with a slight fade, toward the hole. The ball hit the green and rolled to about five feet from the pin. I was so awestruck at having hit a green in regulation that I missed the putt. Nevertheless, my first "real" par left me with such a great feeling. I had a genuine sense of accomplishment and hope for what could be if I kept trying to learn the game. Suddenly, all those things I didn't like about golf didn't matter. I wanted to go back out and play some more, but I was already late for dinner.

Since that time, I've spent the last twenty-plus years learning everything I could about golf: the mechanics of the swing, playing strategy, rules, the history of the game, fashion, etiquette, you name it. I still learn something new about the game almost every day, but this book is an attempt to give you what I, and countless other players, never had—a real guide to all those things no one seems to want to tell you about but you're expected to know. Think of this book as an owner's manual. No more worrying about what to do. If you're not sure, look it up. The answer is probably somewhere in this book.

Even better, these answers are coming from the most famous names in golf, having been taken from over fifty years of their contributions to *Golf Digest.* Names such as Nelson, Mickelson, Ballesteros, Leadbetter, Jenkins, and Sorenstam will tell you how to be a golfer. Also included are contributions from the *Golf Digest* staff of writers, teachers, and equipment experts—even our Mr. Style, Marty Hackel.

You'll notice that in many instances the instruction is gender-specific and also tailored to right-handed players. While *Golf Digest* certainly isn't trying to alienate women or lefties, I felt it important to preserve as much as possible the way the item was originally printed in *Golf Digest.* Since *GD* is largely read by men who swing the club right-handed, most of the instruction was written addressing them. Still, almost all the advice is sound whether you are a man or a woman, a lefty or a righty, a single-digit handicapper or a newbie.

In looking back over the volumes of great how-to stories in *Golf Digest,* I was amazed to find how much of the advice was timeless. The way the game is played and the things you should know about golf have changed very little over the years. In addition to items on swing mechanics, playing strategy, rules, and etiquette, I've also thrown in helpful tips to guide you through a minefield of things that can make the culture of golf initially so intimidating. And, to lighten things up, I've sprinkled some humorous items throughout the chapters.

We realize that the pages of *Golf Digest* can make golf seem so intricate and serious, but in truth the editors here have never forgotten that it's a game. It should be fun, and the pursuit of golf knowledge should seem more like an adventure than a chore. Whenever I see a golfer getting frustrated, I like to recite a couple of lines from one of my favorite movies: *Animal House.*

PINTO: I've gotta work on my game.

OTTER: No, no, no. Don't think of it as work. The point is just to enjoy yourself.

Amen.

RON KASPRISKE

What's a Golfer to Do?

Full-Swing Instruction

When you consider how many books, videos, Web sites, magazines, and academies are devoted to golf instruction, it's probably safe to say no athletic endeavor is more difficult to master. According to the National Golf Foundation, less than 5 percent of all players can shoot lower than eighty! And while seventy-nine is a landmark achievement for a recreational golfer, it's far from good enough to make a living at the sport.

That's why this chapter, devoted to explaining the golf swing, is the longest in the book. And these tips are coming not from the local pro but from several of the greatest players and teachers in the history of the game. Their instruction has been honed over years of studying the swing and backed up by the example of their ability to wield a club.

When you read the tips that follow, keep in mind that there's more than one way to swing a club, so the advice might seem contradictory. What worked for Lee Trevino certainly wouldn't have worked for Ben Hogan. While the physics of the golf swing are scientific fact, teaching the golf swing is an art form.

1 How to construct a golf swing

When you pull that club out of the bag for the first time, you can hone a fundamentally sound golf swing by following these simple steps:

1. Take the address position correctly, with the ball midway between the feet.

2. Lift the club upward with the arms and wrists until the hands are opposite the face.

3. Turn the body to the right, with the arms extended to the correct top-of-swing position.

4. Turn the body to the left until the hands are in the correct finishing position.

—HARVEY PENICK

2 How to take a golf lesson

The process carelessly referred to as "taking a golf lesson" is a fascinating human learning experience. There are some ways you, as a golf student, can participate more fully in your golf lesson. Among those are:

1. Decide in advance what you want out of the lesson.

2. Tell the pro what your problem areas are.

3. If you don't understand what the pro says, ask him or her to explain.

4. Jot down notes about your lesson either during or after.

5. Try to discover how you learn best. Is it by feel, by watching others, or by step-by-step mechanical-like instruction?

6. Try to recite back to the pro just what he has told you.

7. Don't expect a miracle of the professional, or of yourself.

—BETSY RAWLS

3 How a heavy object can teach you golf

The golf swing might seem like a complicated mix of shifting and turning, but you already know how to do it. Take a heavy object (such as a medicine ball), stand sideways, and toss it underhand to a friend. The ball's weight will force you to use your arms and your lower body to get enough power.

The swing works the same way: instead of using the clubhead to lift the ball, use your arms and lower body to generate speed and make a powerful strike on the back of the ball as you move through to your left side. —RANDY SMITH

4 How to diagnose your swing faults from your divots

When you start hitting balls off turf (I know many of you know only those artificial-grass mats on the driving range), take a look at the crater you made in the ground to determine if you are making a sound swing.

• The outside-in divot: If you sliced a shot or pulled it left, your divot mark will point to the left of the target.

• The on-line divot: If you hit the ball straight, the divot will be on your target line and start just after where the ball lay.

• The inside-out divot: If you hooked a shot or pushed it right, your divot mark will point to the right of the target.

• The fat divot: You hit the ground before you hit the ball.

—GARY PLAYER

THE GRIP

5 How to tell from your golf glove if your grip is faulty

Having a gap between your right thumb and index finger can cause the club's handle to slide at the top of the backswing. The left hand can't keep the handle in place by itself, and the sliding causes friction marks on the thumb and palm of many players' gloves. A better right-hand grip position closes the gap and supports the club much better at the top of the backswing. The right wrist stays in a great position this way too. —RANDY SMITH

6 How to find the correct grip pressure

How important is grip pressure to hitting solid shots? I've found that incorrect grip pressure is the most overlooked power leak in the swing. If you grip the club too tightly, your hands aren't free enough to set the correct angles in the backswing; grip it too loosely and they're likely to bend too much and produce a floppy swing motion. To get an idea of how much grip pressure is just right, think of holding a small child's hand. You should do the same with a club. Remember that you have to maintain that same grip pressure throughout the whole swing. —TODD ANDERSON

7 How grip pressure improves your swing

Here's a simple idea that has helped me groove my ball-striking over the years: take a relaxed grip on the club with your right hand. Too much tension in the right hand is the kiss of death in the golf swing. For more consistency at impact and a better release through the ball, keep your right hand passive and let it just go along for the ride.

—AMY ALCOTT

8 How to improve your grip for only a quarter

In high school, I used to make my lunch money by pitching quarters at lunch break. For extra touch, I held the quarter lightly in my fingers. Well, that same fine-touch principle holds true in golf. I always liked the grips on my clubs to be thin so I could hold the club in my fingers. That encouraged touch: the ability to tweak the position of the clubface at the last second through impact. The big-muscle swing taught today doesn't allow that. —JOHNNY MILLER

9 How to use your knuckles to check your grip

You might have heard that you should take your grip so that the Vs (the creases between your thumbs and index fingers) point to your right shoulder. Instead, line up your knuckles on the bottom of the grip. Concentrate on lining up the second knuckles of your fingers. This will allow you to keep the clubface square. —TOM NESS

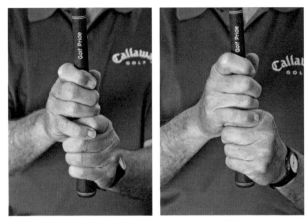

No   Yes

10   How to suck in your chin to improve your posture

Many amateurs struggle with the address position because they've been told to "keep your head down." This can cause you to slouch and can compromise the quality of your balance and motion throughout the swing.

Standing tall and in balance is the foundation of athletic posture. A good spine angle at address starts with setting your head correctly. Pulling in your chin slightly keeps the head in line with the spine and encourages you to look at the ball at the correct angle. It sets the shoulder blades so your back stays straight. If it feels a little awkward at first, it's probably correct. — DAVID LEADBETTER

11   How to adjust your setup from irons to drivers

The fundamentals of addressing a golf ball change slightly depending on the club you are using. With a driver, you are trying to catch the ball slightly on the upswing, to launch it off the tee with the proper trajectory and optimum spin rate. With your irons, you want to

full-swing instruction

squeeze the ball against the turf with a descending blow. So for a driver, tee the ball high and position it forward, just inside your left heel (opposite). Angle your spine away from the target, with the left hip slightly higher than the right. For an iron, play the ball farther back (a hair in front of middle; above). Set your spine angle so it's nearly vertical; feel as if your chest is over the ball.

— DAVID LEADBETTER

TAKEAWAY

12 How to complete your backswing

To get the feel of a full backswing, take your setup with a 5-iron, then rest the shaft of the club on your right shoulder. Turn your back so that it's facing the target, with the club still on your shoulder. Now raise your hands in the air so your left arm is extended. That's exactly where you want to be at the top. Do the opposite to feel a full follow-through. Take your setup and rest the club on your left shoulder. Turn your chest to face the target. Now raise your hands, extending your right arm. That's your finish. — RICK SMITH

13 How your wrinkles can help your swing

To make sure you're starting the backswing correctly, check the wrinkles on your wrists. When the club gets parallel to the ground, your left wrist should be flat at the spot where your watch would rest, and you should see wrinkles on the back of your right wrist. The most common mistake is to bend both wrists up, which can change the path of the swing and lead to poor contact. — TOM NESS

14 How to feel the correct backswing

Since feel is so important in the swing, it is imperative that a golfer promote it from the start. The very first movement I make is the forward press. The backswing, as Ben Hogan said, is a "rebound" from the forward press. As I start back, my hands feel together, and I make a conscious effort to swing smoothly, keeping the clubhead low by almost dragging it along the ground. I swing as far back as I can without straining, and at the top of the backswing my chin is directly over my left shoulder. —ARNOLD PALMER

15 How to spot your backswing flaws

I spend a lot of time swinging into the correct backswing position, then verifying it by checking in a mirror. When you do this, the shaft should be on a line parallel with your left arm as you get toward the top (keep in mind that it will look like your right arm in the mirror). Also, make sure your right elbow stays tucked to your side.

—STEVE STRICKER

DOWNSWING

16 How to transition from backswing to downswing

A split second before completing the backswing, the best players make a slight lateral move toward the target with their hips and trunk. This move not only allows the arms to swing down on plane but helps increase swing speed by providing improved leverage between the body and the club. It's a real power move.

If you want to copy it, first train with my step drill. On the range, grab a 7-iron, tee up a ball, and address it with a narrow stance. Your front foot should be in line with the ball. Take the club to the top, but before you start down, step toward the target with your front foot. This action will help you feel that lateral move and put some power into your golf swing.   —RICK SMITH

17 How to start your downswing

Opinions vary about how to swing down from the top. Some say you turn your hips back to the left. Others say the downswing begins with a downward pull of the left hand and arm. Still others say it starts with a lowering of the left heel.

Since you can think of only one thing at a time while swinging a golf club, choose whichever reminder helps you start down without prematurely uncocking the wrists. My belief is that the downswing starts when my left hip turns and leads the way, with the rest of me going along as a package.   —SAM SNEAD

18 How to hit shots more solidly

What every pro golfer does, to some degree, is try to maintain lag through impact. This is the only way to compress the ball with the club and hit a solid shot, but amateurs often allow the clubhead to get ahead of the hands as the club hits the ball.

I can't stress enough the importance of keeping your hands ahead of the clubhead (which is lag) for as long as you can, down and through the shot. You might have been told to "release the club," but to me the only way to release the club is to throw it down the fairway. Instead of that notion, you need to maintain a "hands-ahead" position well into the through swing. Think about your hands staying ahead of the clubhead well past impact.   —ROB AKINS

TEMPO

19 How to determine your swing speed

Grab a 5-iron, tee some balls, and hit practice shots with a narrow stance, the sides of your feel literally touching. This forces you to swing the club freely with your arms. If your shoulders take over, you'll lose your balance.

Once you start making solid contact, you'll be amazed how far you can hit the ball with your feet together. You'll note the sensation of the arms swinging freely and your shoulders turning easily. Your backswing will feel much slower and freer.

Try to duplicate these sensations as you gradually widen your stance and allow your legs to become more active.   —BOB TOSKI

20 How to count your way to a better tempo

I seldom hit a shot very hard or very soft. To set your tempo, try my one-two-three practice swing. Count one-two-three as you swing to the top, then one-two-three to the finish. Count at the same rate going back and coming down, and this will keep your tempo even and your swing speed in check. — ANNIKA SORENSTAM

21 How to hit the ball like "The Big Easy"

Instead of trying to rip every shot as far as I can, I consciously make about a three-quarter effort, maybe 85 percent at the max. I've found that I get more distance that way, because my transition from backswing to downswing is better and my mechanics don't get out of whack. Focus on turning completely through the shot to a full finish. Without worrying about speeding up the clubhead with your hands or arms, you'll get all the distance you need. — ERNIE ELS

full-swing instruction

15

How to be a politically correct golfer

I don't know what you've been doing lately, but I've been studiously preparing for how I'm going to handle it when political correctness comes to golf. This could be any moment now, depending on the winds that are being blown earthward by various lofty idealists, none of whom can cure a slice.

Oddly enough, I still come across the occasional person who doesn't understand what political correctness means. Here it is: politically correct advocates see a short person as being vertically impaired. When I first heard this, I immediately thought of how utterly tasteless it was of so many sportswriters to refer to Ben Hogan as Bantam Ben or the Wee Ice Mon. The ugly insinuations here were obvious—Ben Hogan was shorter than some people!

I thought of how the politically correct correspondent at the 1953 British Open might have written his lead: "Differently sized Ben Hogan, the Vertically Impaired Ice Mon, finished the British Open today with a score that was in variance with others in the field. While no competitor actually lost the golf tournament, and while this tournament was no more important than any other, the trophy was awarded to Hogan on the basis of a general opinion that fewer of his tee shots wound up in the taller growth regions at Carnoustie."

I can think of numerous words that will get you in trouble when PC creeps into golf, such as *slice, hook, rough, bunker, handicap,* and *shank.* Instead of them . . .

Hook: A shot that is leftward-prone.
Wild off the tee: Shots are diversified.
Shanked shot: Laterally extravagant shot.
Ball in the water: Nonaquatic ball.
Miss a putt: Ask too much of the cup size.

—DAN JENKINS

22　How to swing smoothly

Tour players swing at about 80 to 85 percent of their maximum speed. They know that any faster and they start to lose control. To find your ideal tempo, tee a ball just off the ground and set up to it with your 5-iron. Raise the clubhead over the ball and swing the club a few feet toward the target. Without stopping, reverse direction and go back over the ball and into your normal swing, hitting the shot. You'll be amazed how smooth you feel through impact.　　—BUTCH HARMON

23　How to get your rhythm and distance control back at the same time

Whenever I feel like my tempo is off and I'm hitting the same club inconsistent distances, I drop nine practice balls on the ground and, using my 7-iron, start by hitting three balls softly. Next, I hit three more balls, this time with medium speed. Finally, I hit three balls as hard as I can without losing my balance. Try it. You'll learn that an easy 7-iron goes as far as a hard 8-iron.　　—LORENA OCHOA

full-swing instruction

24 How to swing as smoothly as me

People always ask me about my tempo: how do I hit the ball so long when I look like I'm swinging in slow motion? I don't know the secret to good tempo, but I do know that when I want to really smash one, I start out nice and easy and accumulate speed as I go.

Power comes from swinging your fastest at the point of impact, and for me that means staying loose and letting the speed build. A rhythmic backswing helps me make a full turn, and starting down softly lets me match up my body, my arms, and the club through impact. My feet are very quiet. I don't make any violent moves on the way down. — FRED COUPLES

25 How to step into a better weight shift

The proper sequence of motion in going from backward to forward is a dynamic all good athletes have. It allows you to transfer the energy created with coil and torque.

To ingrain the correct sequence, practice raising your left foot before you swing to the top. As you complete your windup, feel as if you're already "stepping into" your swing. This double-directional move promotes a better weight shift, helps brace your legs as you change direction, and encourages you to begin the downswing with your lower body. — DAVID LEADBETTER

26 Another way to improve your weight shift

I'm trying to get my hips to rotate more instead of sliding on the downswing. Amateurs have this problem too, and often slice because the hips move laterally instead of rotating. You have to rotate to swing a baseball bat, so hitting a ball off a baseball tee really helps give me the feeling of clearing my left side. This drill also helps me produce a more shallow approach to the ball. It's also fun to do. —CHARLES HOWELL

27 How to prevent your body from swaying

Swaying occurs when your body moves laterally to your right on your backswing instead of coiling or winding around a central axis. Most often, swaying causes the weight to shift to the outside of the right foot on the backswing.

Don't try to correct a sway by keeping most of the weight on the left foot. Keeping the weight to the left prevents a full hip turn and unnecessarily restricts your backswing.

To prevent swaying, simply make sure that ample pressure is maintained on the inside portion of your right foot. This will help you coil, instead of sway, your body as you swing the club back.

— JIMMY DEMARET

28 How to hit it on the driver's sweet spot

Where the clubhead contacts the ball is the most important factor in determining the starting direction of any shot. Ideally, you want the club to approach the ball from inside the target line and make contact on the back of the ball. To do this, transfer your weight to your left leg on the downswing. I initiate this shift by pushing off the inside of my right foot. This gets my hands slightly ahead of the ball at impact and brings the club into the back of the ball from the inside.

—HANK HANEY

Yes   No

29 How to hit it 10 yards farther

When I want extra distance, I make a bigger shoulder turn, which gives me more time to generate speed on the downswing. More important, I make sure not to get lazy with my leg action on the downswing. You want to feel like you're throwing your legs at the target while staying steady. That's how I get good hip turn and hit 300-yard drives.

—ERNIE ELS

30 Two more keys to a 10-yard increase in driving

Make a fuller turn and maintain a relaxed grip pressure throughout the swing. Be sure to complete your backswing to maximize your coil. And the relaxed grip pressure ensures good clubhead release for increased clubhead speed.

—DAVID LEADBETTER

31 How to improve your power with your arc

A wide arc is a must for achieving both distance and accuracy in golf shots. It's more than just trying to keep the left arm straight and reaching high with the hands at the top of the backswing. The only move I consciously try to make to obtain a wider arc is to stretch my left arm and the muscles of my left side on the backswing. As you stretch, your left shoulder should turn under your chin.

— MICKEY WRIGHT

32 How to squeeze all of the power out of your body

Many golfers, especially women, simply do not allow the lower body to participate freely in the swing. Swinging almost exclusively with the arms and shoulders, they sacrifice distance, a commodity most players would welcome.

My advice on how to get all of your power into the act is to adopt a "shoulder-to-shoulder" swing. That is, concentrate on swinging the hands to a point over the right shoulder on the backswing, then to a point over the left shoulder at the finish. If the club is swung in this manner, the golfer's body will react properly without further concern. The lower-body muscles will automatically loosen and help with the swing. More clubhead speed and greater distance will result.

— KATHY WHITWORTH

full-swing instruction

33 How to be sneaky long

Size-wise, I'm no monster. But when I have to, I can drive a golf ball far. I'm what you call "sneaky long." The key is the right elbow. If your elbow is almost flush against your right hip through impact, you'll have power to burn. You'll sense power in your right arm, like a boxer about to throw a punch. —LEE TREVINO

How to tell if you need another golf instructor

Finding a golf instructor is easy. Finding a good golf instructor isn't. Here are some warning signs you might need to make a change:

- He asks if you'd rather have your swing videotaped in Betamax or VHS.
- Part of your golf lesson includes waxing his car and painting his fence.
- He claims he's the "fifth Harmon brother."
- His only instruction book: *How I Turned Ian Baker-Finch's Game Around.*
- After your lesson, he asks if he can bum a ride home.
- When you ask for a tip to cure your slice, he says, "Are you familiar with shock therapy?"
- He pauses in midspeech and looks around every time he hears a siren.
- He cautions you not to hit too many balls because it will take you too long to shag them.
- You ask him who influenced his teaching style and he replies, "Why? What did you hear?"
- Every time he watches you swing, he stands behind your back.

—RON KASPRISKE

34 How to add 30 yards off the tee

EDITOR'S NOTE: *A thirty-yard gain might seem far-fetched, but Gary Player claims to have done that back in 1960 when he won the Masters. He was hitting it thirty yards farther than he did the previous year, he said. Here are the things he did, and you can do, to make tremendous yardage gains.*

• I had all of my clubs made a half-inch longer than standard length. Longer clubs are going to give you a longer swing arc, and if you have a longer swing arc, you're automatically going to hit the ball farther.

• I improved my weight shift. I always had problems shifting my weight to my left foot on the downswing. The only thing I concentrate on during my swing is shifting my weight to the left foot when returning the clubhead to the ball.

• I delay the uncocking of the wrists. This is the real secret of long drives. You should be conscious of your hands and arms in the golf swing. If you shift your weight forward immediately on the downswing, you will get your delayed uncocking automatically.

• I close my stance so that my right foot is pulled farther back than my left. It is easier for me to get a full body turn on the backswing. By doing so, you add both rhythm and power to your swing.

• I want the right elbow tucked into my side as soon as possible on the downswing. This is also true of my right leg. Bringing the right elbow in tight to the body and kicking the right knee toward the target first thing on the downswing will help you get your weight onto your left foot. —GARY PLAYER

35 How to learn to swing harder without hurting yourself

EDITOR'S NOTE: *Jason Zuback is a former World Long Drive champion.*

Because the body prefers the comfort of the same old routine, it doesn't like a change that requires expending more energy. Increasing your clubhead speed demands change, however. But you can trick the body into producing more speed by swinging something light or something heavy. Here's how to go about that. First, I'll grip a 5-iron by the head and try to swing the shaft as fast as I can on the downswing. I'll alternate between the right hand and the left, keeping my feet together to start and then stepping through on the finish. Make sure that the swoosh the shaft makes through the air is loudest at the bottom of your swing.

Second, I sometimes swing a weighted club to get stronger and swing harder. When I do, the additional weight should be relatively light. Otherwise, I might inadvertently use muscle groups that I don't use for swinging my driver. I can develop all the swing speed I need just by duct-taping a golf ball to the head of an iron.

— JASON ZUBACK

36 How to hit your fairway woods farther

Many of you are intimidated by the thought of using the woods in your bag. Chances are you have an erroneous concept of the swing. When preparing for a drive, many golfers have all kinds of strange thoughts running through their heads. As they check their grip and stance, some sort of golf gremlin keeps saying, "You're really going to hit this. You're going to put everything you have into the swing and really send the ball sailing!" What happens? In getting all keyed up for this extra-long drive, the golfer becomes tense and then, disregarding all rhythm and smoothness, puts an overdose of power into the swing. The result is bad. The point is that there is no percentage in pressing wood shots. If you will just be content to let the clubhead do the work and settle for the best distance within the limits of your physical capabilities, you will score much better.

— BABE ZAHARIAS

37 How to use your knees to gain distance off the tee

One way to gain some power is to focus on the lower body. I want you to maintain a feeling of a soft right leg on the downswing. This requires you to flex the right knee slightly at address and increase that flex as the club swings down. Your knee should be pointing at the target line in front of the ball as the club approaches impact. This promotes a more powerful swing through the ball and greater distance off the tee.

— JIM MCLEAN

38 How to hit big drives as you get older

Those of us moving into our twilight years have no problem getting to Denny's before 5 p.m. But what we can't do is make a full turn on the backswing like Tiger Woods. That means we can't hit the ball as far, right?

Well, not exactly. You can make a full backswing by allowing your left knee to turn and point behind the ball. This helps you make a bigger shoulder turn and sets up a powerful downswing, because the club will have more time to pick up speed as it approaches the ball.

—GARY MCCORD

39 How to smash it like a baseball slugger

Back in the 1970s, I was the head professional at Losantiville Country Club in Cincinnati. That's where I met Johnny Bench. Bench told me that when he swung for the fences, he held the bat lighter to increase his bat speed.

The same principle applies to golf. A light grip pressure, with your arms relaxed at address and throughout the swing, allows you to release the club freely and with full extension.   —JIM FLICK

40 How to make a powerful downswing

The most important part of the golf swing in terms of hitting a powerful shot is the transition from backswing to downswing. Try my "SpongeBob" drill on the practice tee to hone a better move. Place a thick, rectangular sponge under your left foot. As you turn back, you should feel some pressure on the sponge. But as you change direction and swing down, the pressure should increase dramatically—in other words, squash the sponge! To do that, your lower body has to move forward in the correct fashion, transferring tremendous energy into your arms and the club and setting you up for a booming drive.

—DAVID LEADBETTER

41 How to tilt your body to hit it longer

Spine tilt is one of the most misunderstood and least appreciated parts of the swing. For instance, with the driver, big hitters tilt their spines approximately ten degrees away from the target at address. But at impact they tilt back twice as much.

In order to increase your distance off the tee, shift your weight forward and rotate your hips toward the target in the downswing, which will change your original spine angle. When you push off your right side and rotate, the lower part of your spine shifts forward while the upper part tips farther away from the target, effectively doubling the tilt from address. — JIM MCLEAN

42 How to hinge the wrists for power

Hand-wrist action constitutes the most important factor in a golf swing. There are two things I want to happen at the top of the backswing:

1. The toe of the clubhead should point at the ground.

2. The wrists should be fully cocked and under the shaft. Properly and fully cocked, the wrists are now in a position to remain cocked until near impact and thus apply their full power.

Here's how to do this two-step drill: Address an imaginary ball as though you were going to hit a shot. Then lift the clubhead straight up in front of you by bending your wrists as much as you can. Keeping this position, swing your arms up and around to the top of your backswing. This is the correct wrist-hand position.

— PATTY BERG

43 How to be the longest player in your foursome

There's an expression in golf known as "sneaky long." It means people don't expect you to be able to crush a drive (too small, too old, too inexperienced) but you somehow manage to outdrive everyone. Here are some tips so you can be that person in your foursome.

• Hit it with all your weight behind the strike. To do this, tee the ball under your left shoulder joint. Then make a downswing where the club bottoms under that joint.

• Flare the front foot at address. This will help you swing through the ball, particularly if you have a lower-back or hip problem.

• As you take the club back, the arms and chest should move as one. Staying in sync like this promotes a wider, slower turn and allows you to build power.

• When you start the downswing, feel as if your body turn pulls the club down.

• Stay balanced throughout the swing. Swing too hard and you'll lose your balance and won't hit the ball on the sweet spot.

—STUART APPLEBY

full-swing instruction

44 What you should think about when you want to bomb it

Driving it a long way has always come natural to me. One thought that has helped me with the driver is "smash it." I don't mean swing hard. I try to compress the ball with a dead-solid hit. That image works at any swing speed. — FRED COUPLES

ACCURACY

45 How to pure your irons

Most great iron players have at least one thing in common: they take a divot, whether the ball is teed up or on the turf. And the angle of attack is usually shallow, which produces a long, shallow divot about the size of a dollar bill. To improve your ball striking, try shallowing out your backswing by swinging a little more around you. This sets up a narrow angle into the ball and a long, thin divot. It also helps if you turn the knuckles of your top hand toward the ground through impact. This is a clear sign that you're compressing the ball, trapping it between the clubface and the turf, which will result in a divot on the forward side of the ball. — TIGER WOODS

46 How to check your aim

Here's an alignment drill I use when I practice. Take your address, then lay the club down against your heels—which is more accurate than using your toes. Step behind the ball and see where the shaft is pointing. For straight shots, it should be parallel to your target line (picture a railroad track).

Matching your hips and shoulders to your heel line is the best way I know to set good alignment. —ANNIKA SORENSTAM

47 How to hit straighter drives

Straight driving enabled me to win two U.S. Opens, and for the amateur player the premium on straight driving is just as important. Even if the rough isn't severe, you still usually wind up making bogeys because you're not playing the holes the way they were designed to be played.

I learned a long time ago how to keep my ball in play when I really need to. My method is simple and highly repeatable. Try it.

1. Strengthen your grip and aim left. Try to keep the clubhead traveling down the target line for as long as possible. The one danger is leaving the clubface open and hitting a weak block or slice to the right. The secret is to strengthen your right-hand grip

so that, at address, the V formed by the right thumb and forefinger points to the right of your right shoulder. That will help you rotate the clubface naturally to a square position at impact.

2. Keep the clubface square for as long as possible through impact. To accomplish this, let your left arm come away from your side on the follow-through, with the club extending down the target line for as long as possible. Don't worry about squaring the clubface by rotating it. The strong right-hand grip will take care of that.

—LEE TREVINO

48 How to fish your way to better accuracy

I've spent more than my share of time on a bass boat, and when I cast my fishing rod the movement of my elbow is exactly the one I want to use in a golf swing.

To cast a fishing rod correctly, you move your elbow down and keep it ahead of the handle of the pole. That makes the tip end move fast and the lure fly far and straight. Here's how to apply this technique to your golf swing.

1. When you make your backswing, the right elbow has to bend at the top. Without that ninety-degree angle, the wrists can't cock the right way.

2. On the downswing, feel like your right elbow is swinging down at the ball first. Don't let that elbow drift up and away.

—RANDY SMITH

49 How to hit it down the middle

The best ball-strikers have the club on plane going back so they don't have to reroute it to get it on plane coming down.

To check your swing plane, imagine two panes of glass: one fitted above your midsection and the other on your shoulders. The space between those two panes creates a slot for your backswing. My left arm, my shoulders, and the shaft are virtually on the same plane. I achieve this by avoiding the imaginary glass on either side. From this position, you are set to hit the ball in the center of the clubface.   —JOSH ZANDER

50 How to shape your tee shots by changing your tee height

I don't want to make any shot harder than it has to be. When I hit my driver, I always start from the same basic setup, then make subtle adjustments to get the ball flight I want.

For my normal tee shot—a high, slight draw—I tee it high, so that about half the ball extends over the top of my driver. The high tee makes it easier to close the clubface through impact. Then I think about swinging more around my body for a draw.

For a fade, I tee the ball about a half-inch lower and think about finishing the swing with the arms in a more extended position. The lower tee makes it easier to hit down with a slightly open face.

Most important, regardless of tee height, I never change my grip.

—ERNIE ELS

51   How to find the fairway

When you start spraying your tee shots, try this three-step approach to straightening things out.

1. Strengthen your grip. The key for me is to feel the thumb pad on my left hand covering the top of the grip.

2. Stand wider. This discourages side-to-side movement of the hips. If the hips slide, it's easy to slice.

3. To get a feel for proper shoulder position at impact, try this drill: Hold out your left hand, swing back your right hand, then slap your left. Your hands should meet directly in front of you. If your shoulders are open—a slice position—your hands will meet too far forward. Strive for a feeling of square shoulders at impact.   —ANNIKA SORENSTAM

52   How to cure an over-the-top move

To improve your swing path to the ball and cure the "over-the-top" move—swinging from outside to inside the intended line of flight—simply "swing across your lap." To do this, keep the right elbow moving close to the right hip as it crosses the lap on the downswing. This puts the club on the proper track—from inside to along the target line.   —PEGGY KIRK BELL

53 How to hit long irons for accuracy

EDITOR'S NOTE: *If you haven't made the switch to hybrids and still carry a 2-, 3-, or 4-iron, follow this timeless advice from Ben Hogan on how to use those clubs properly.*

If there is any great difference between an iron shot and a wood shot, it is that an iron shot is definitely a sharp hit, while a wood shot is swung and the ball is swept off either the tee or the turf. Since the iron swing is shorter than the wood swing, and because the player must hit down on the ball, the action of the body and the hands must be speeded up considerably. Here are some tips:

• Set the wrists much sooner in the backswing than you do with a wood. This enables you to hit down and through the ball.

• Shift your weight to the left foot at the top of your swing. Do it much sooner and faster than you do with a wood.

• The first movement in the downswing for the long iron is the turning of the left hip to the left.

• Hitting down is an important part of iron play.

• Hit the ball as if you were driving it forward.

—BEN HOGAN

54 How to square the clubface at impact

Your forearms play an important role in squaring the clubface at impact. If your forearms are rotating as the body turns through the shot, your wrists will uncock naturally and your chances for solid contact and a straight shot will greatly improve.

To improve your forearm rotation, swing your club halfway back and then halfway through, with the toe of the club pointing up at each position. This mini swing will give you the feeling of proper forearm rotation. — JUDY RANKIN

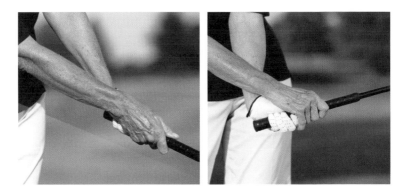

55 How to align yourself to the target

At address, you should aim the clubface exactly where you want the ball to start. A lot of amateurs make the mistake of aiming the body first. Good players begin by aiming the clubface first—about the same moment they "step into the shot" with the right foot. Here's the best way to set up: Examine the target closely, then look down to make sure the clubface is aimed exactly on the line where you want the ball to begin its flight. Only then do you place your left foot in position and make the final adjustments with your feet and shoulders.

— BUTCH HARMON

56 How to use the wrists to square the club at impact

No matter how you swing the club through impact, keep your lead wrist flat. The clubface mirrors the wrist, so flat means square. Keeping it flat also maintains the extension in your swing for solid contact and power.

—CHUCK COOK

57 How to hit a high fairway wood

To hit a high fairway wood, you should stand quite close to the ball at address. This will put your swing on an upright plane so that you can take full advantage of the club's loft at impact. Also, keep your weight well back on your heels. This helps you turn in balance and keeps your body behind the ball. Picture where you want the ball to finish, and then take the club straight back from the ball in line with the target. On the downswing, if you try to return the club along this same target line, you will be amazed how straight you can actually hit the shot. After the club goes straight back from the ball for two or three inches, it should begin its move upward. Aided by a full turn of the shoulders, your hands should move to a high position above your shoulders. This high hand position is important because the club should move into the ball at a more downward angle. It is not necessary to scoop or sweep the ball into flight.

—BYRON NELSON

58 How to cure a slice

To cure a slice, check to see:

- That the clubhead starts back inside the target line.
- That the left side is completing the turn, with the weight shifted against the right leg.
- That the left hand and arm are dominating the backswing and the start of the downswing.
- That the stance is not one used for the intentional slice, which hinders a complete pivot.

For a quick cure, attempt to hit the ball to the right of the fairway. This will aid in bringing the clubhead into the ball from the inside. —SAM SNEAD

59 Five more ways to cure your slice

Tired of seeing your shots curve way right of the target? To get that banana ball flying straight again, try these tips:

1. Drop your right foot back about twelve inches at address and practice hitting drives with your normal swing.

2. Instead of gripping the club normally, take your driver and grip it as if it were a baseball bat, with a slight separation between the hands. Hit some tee shots with this grip.

3. Keeping the split-hand grip, set the clubhead on the ground about four feet behind the ball, well inside the target line. From this position, swing the clubhead over the ball and all the way to the finish. Feel as if you're making a low-to-high sweeping motion with forearm rotation. After practicing this for a while, tee the ball extra high and hit drives with half-swings, trying to produce a slight draw.

4. At address, hold your driver with your right hand and put your left

hand on the front of your right shoulder. Swing with the right arm only, focusing on pushing your right shoulder out of the way on the backswing and swinging your right arm past your body to the finish.

5. Stick a stake or shaft in the ground about five yards behind you on an extension of your foot line. With your eyes on the stake, practice making backswings that start slightly outside the stake, and then drop the club inside the stake on the downswing. There's no need to hit balls.

— RICK SMITH

1   2   3

4   5

60 How to fix a slice while sitting down

Ninety percent of the golfers I teach fear losing the ball to the right. Nearly all tour players fear losing it left. The chair drill cures both fears.

Simply swing a club while sitting in a chair. Focus on your left forearm: turn it freely, with the clubface turning down after "impact" to eliminate those weak slices.

This drill will eliminate the flip by keeping the body quiet so your hands and arms can control the clubhead to create your desired ball flight.   — JIM FLICK

61 How to address the ball to cure a slice

Golfers who hit a weak slice have two basic problems: they cut across the ball with an out-to-in swing path, and they have an open clubface at impact.

You can eliminate one of these problems from the start by turning the clubface closed before you take your grip. To set the club in the same position every time, hold it in front of your chest and visualize

an imaginary clockface. Rotate the toe from twelve o'clock (square) to eleven o'clock (closed). Do not grip the club and then turn the toe to 11 o'clock, since that's just rotating your hands without closing the face.

Once your shots start to consistently curve to the left, you'll adjust to your new ball flight and stop swinging out to in, thus curing the other part of the problem. — DAVID LEADBETTER

62 How to fix a slice with your right elbow

You hear a lot about tour players "getting stuck" on the downswing. This refers to the right elbow getting too far behind the right hip late in the downswing. Amateurs typically have the opposite problem: a right elbow that's too far from the right hip on the downswing and causes that big, nasty slice. This move is evidence of an outside-to-in swing path and usually results in a finish in which the left arm saws across the chest.

To fix this fault, swing to the top, then bring the club down into what I call the "delivery position." The shaft should be parallel to or slightly inside the target line as it nears the halfway-down position. Focus on keeping the right elbow close to, but in front of, the right hip as you swing down. — JIM McLEAN

63 How to cure a hook

A shot that unintentionally curves severely from right to left is easily cured with these tips:

• Weaken your left-hand position so the left thumb points straight down the shaft, instead of down the right side.

• Open your stance so the left foot is drawn back slightly.

• Swing a little more upright.

• Stay "under" the shot more by keeping the clubhead moving toward the target for as long as possible. —BILLY CASPER

64 How to fade it into the fairway

To hit a fade, I make two adjustments to my setup. First, I aim as far left of the target as I want the ball to start. Second, I open the clubface, pointing it to where I want the ball to land. Then I make my normal swing. —LORENA OCHOA

65 How to stop pushing tee shots

If you are hitting shots that consistently fly on a straight path right of your target, you are hitting a push. Here are a couple of ways to cure it.

1. Tee up a ball and narrow your stance, with your feet twelve inches apart. Try hitting some drives like this. The narrow stance will make your lower body less likely to turn aggressively on the downswing. You want to feel your arms swinging down and releasing past your body.

2. A good release keeps the ball from going right. If the arms and wrists are tense, they block the natural rotation and release of the club. To test your tension, hold the club up in front of you and make circles in the air using only your wrists. If your wrists are loose, it'll be easy to do. —BUTCH HARMON

1   2

66 How your setup can promote a draw

Making the ball curve from right to left is as simple as changing your setup. Make sure your eyes, shoulders, hips, and knees are parallel to the target line. Then move your right foot back, closing your stance (or foot line) so that it is pointed slightly to the right of the target. —BOB TOSKI

67 · How to draw a ball by playing handball

The right-to-left ball flight (for righties) is one that many golfers fall in love with. The best way to hit a draw is to visualize that you are playing handball. To curve the ball left, you have to hit it with the palm of your right hand facing the target at impact and then turning left and down as the hand swings through. Now, when you hold the club, visualize your right hand making the same motion.

— JOSH ZANDER

68 Another way to use your hands to hit a draw

If you want to draw the ball, the clubface has to be closed or closing through impact. To do this, your right hand must roll over your left through impact. To get a good mental picture of this action, imagine spilling a bucket of water to your left. — CHUCK COOK

69 How playing pool can help you curve the ball

When you play pool and you want the ball to carom to the right, you hit the left side of it with the cue ball. The same holds true in golf. If you're continually hitting shots left of your target, focus on a dimple on the ball that's inside the target line as you address it. If you hit that dimple, the ball will start right of your target line.

This also narrows your focus and improves your chances of hitting a crisp shot. If you push your shots to the right, hit a dimple that's outside the target line and the ball will start left. —JOSH ZANDER

SOLID SHOTS

70 How to sting your long irons

Most amateurs are intimidated by the long irons because these clubs have straighter faces and smaller heads. The reason I play them well is that my swing with the 2-iron is no different from my swing with the 7-iron.

Make a full shoulder turn, and be certain you complete the backswing before starting down. The start of the downswing is the same as the start of the backswing—go slow. There should be a feeling of pulling down slowly. But as far as I'm concerned, the secret to a successful swing is in the feet. I barely lift my left heel off the ground. I'd recommend you let it come up naturally, but only as far as necessary to make a good turn. On the downswing, I have the feeling I'm driving off the inside of that right foot through the impact area. —TOM WEISKOPF

71 How to hit a hybrid solidly

To use these new clubs correctly, make more of a sweeping stroke. There is plenty of weight behind the head with these clubs, so you don't have to force them. Don't hit down on the ball as you would with an iron. Instead, make a nice, level blow, and don't take a divot. Play the ball where you would for a fairway wood (inside your left heel). —BOB TOSKI

72 How to trick your mind into hitting your long irons better

Swing the long irons as though they all have the number "7" stamped on the sole. If you swing the 3-iron like you do the 7-iron, you won't swing too hard or try to help the ball into the air.

—JACK NICKLAUS

73 How to hit your middle irons better

To play great middle-iron shots, you need traction for action. Playing the ball just forward of center, bend from your hips, so you have a solid base and you feel light on your feet—as if you're ready to spring into action, like a cat about to jump. On the downswing, shift your lower body toward the target, so your hands and arms learn to square the clubface at impact. (Byron Nelson was the best at this.) Lead your middle-iron downswing with your lower body, while keeping your grip pressure light and constant. That will result in a slightly downward angle of attack, promoting solid contact and allowing the club to square up for straighter shots.   —BOB TOSKI

74 How to avoid getting "ball-bound"

On long shots, it's hard to keep the hit impulse under control—known by some as being "ball-bound"—because you feel you need a lot of force to propel the ball a long way. This causes your hands to move into action too soon. To me, a hit is simply the result of the ball getting in the way of the club. Ever notice that your practice swings on the course are generally better than your real swings? That's because there is nothing down there to hit at.

I find that an excellent way to avoid hitting at the ball is to imagine there is a soap bubble down there. Instead of applying excessive force, just try to burst the bubble. Your arms swing down freely. A smooth, properly timed swing will result.   —BOB TOSKI

75 How to hit crisper shots from the fairway

Shots from the fairway should not be thought of as power shots. Don't swing your hands back to twelve o'clock, as you might with a driver. Stop at ten o'clock, and fight the tendency to hang back on your right side and scoop the ball off the ground. Hit down on the ball by making a good shift to your left side.

One thing I do to hit crisp shots is turn my head toward the target before impact to create more forward rotation. It helps me get to my front side and make a downward strike. —ANNIKA SORENSTAM

76 How ice cream can help you stay down through the shot

Some players come up out of their shots too quickly, especially full shots. I focus on getting them to hit down and stay down through the shot—not scoop it.

Speaking of scoop, an image that works well in teaching this notion—especially with kids—is that of an ice cream cone. Imagine that a cone is stuck in the ground like a tee and that the ice cream is the ball. If you were to hit this shot, you wouldn't want to just scoop the ice cream out of the cone. You would need to hit down and into the cone itself, to create a descending blow and solid impact. —RENEE POWELL

77 How to "brush up" on your swing basics

The wrist action you use with a paintbrush is similar to that needed in the golf swing. It's one of the most vivid images we use in golf instruction. The premise is that when you paint, the handle leads the bristles in a loose-wristed motion back and forth. The same holds true in a good swing: the handle leads the clubhead. This is especially true on the downswing, where clubhead lag creates an explosive delivery for a crisp, powerful strike. Next time you hit balls, think about a relaxed-wrist painting motion.　　— JIM MCLEAN

78 How to improve your swing path into the ball

For the best iron-shot results, the clubhead should be swung into the ball on the same low angle that it took at the start of the backswing. The inevitable result of such a swing is a shallow divot in front of the ball's original position. Many golfers, upon hearing that you must hit down on the ball, swing down on an angle that's too steep or abrupt. There is little chance of solidly hitting the back of the ball this way. But if the clubhead follows a low angle into the impact area, you will make sweet contact.　　— DAVIS LOVE JR.

79 How to catch it flush with an iron

The grooves on the upper half of an iron's clubface are useful for alignment, but that's all. If you strike the ball higher than the fifth groove from the bottom, it hardly goes anywhere. There's just not enough mass up there to compress the ball. Keep this in mind when teeing the ball on par 3s. Never tee the ball more than a half-inch above the ground. Any higher and you bring the upper part of the clubface into play. A quarter of an inch is standard.

This so-called dead zone also comes into play when your ball is suspended in tall grass. You can help take the upper part of the clubface out of play by gripping down on the club.

— JOHNNY MILLER

80 How straight should the left arm be to hit it flush?

One of the most common misconceptions about the golf swing is that you should keep your left arm straight as you swing to the top. In fact, a soft left arm, with a little give at the elbow, promotes a more connected swing—the arms and body working together. This is crucial to great ball-striking. — JIM MCLEAN

81 How to stop hitting the ball on the toe of the club

If you're hitting the ball out on the toe of the club, it usually means your arms are losing their extension as the club moves into the impact zone. This generally happens because your swing path is pulling in to help get the ball airborne. To cure this problem, stick two tees in the ground about a clubhead apart. Set up to the tee that's closer to you, but swing at the one farther away. This drill will flatten your downswing path and help you extend your arms. Extension is key. You'll also swing the club around the body, helping to eliminate toe hits. — JIM MCLEAN

82 How to hit it like a tour pro

You might see some variations in the backswings of tour pros, but one aspect of the swing is the same for all of them: their hands are ahead of the clubhead at impact.

Improve your impact position and swing like a tour pro by making some short swings with a 6-iron. Feel as if you're hitting a low punch shot, and really exaggerate the sensation of your hands staying out ahead of the clubhead through the bottom of the swing. This drill will reinforce the idea that you don't have to hit up on the ball to make it fly high. The key to trajectory and distance is compressing the ball with the clubface. — CHUCK COOK

83 How to stop topping your 3-wood

Hitting a 3-wood off a tight fairway lie brings out the worst in a lot of golfers. To make solid contact with a fairway wood, hit with a descending blow, scraping the grass or even taking a small divot. For that to happen, you have to shift your weight to your front side and swing through the ball, letting your arms fully extend. Think about swinging to a full finish and not about hitting the ball. —BUTCH HARMON

84 Why you shouldn't keep your head down

One of the worst clichés I hear is that you've got to keep your head down during the backswing. Too much of that leads to the shoulder bouncing off the chin, creating a shoulder tilt instead of a good shoulder turn.

The same is true through impact. Keeping your head down prevents you from turning through the right way. Instead, let your eyes follow the clubhead as it hits the ball and moves into the follow-through. Synchronize the swing of the club with the turn of your head toward the target. —HANK HANEY

85 How to develop a swing that repeats

There are several fundamentals to a good golf swing that are applicable to everyone. I think anyone can be a 70-shooter, but he has to want to do it—and he must work at it. Here are the fundamentals:

• Grip: The union of the two hands must be right and constant or all else is lost.

• Posture: Right foot straight, left toe pointing out, knees slightly flexed, back straight.

• Arms: From the clubhead to the left shoulder, there should be but one hinge—at the hands. With the left arm firm and the right arm loose, you can be assured of always coming back to the ball in the same place. The right elbow points to the body.

• Swing: The left arm continues to be straight all through the backswing. This permits the clubhead to travel the greatest distance. The right elbow points to the ground at the top of the backswing.

• Follow-through: As you swing through the ball, the right arm straightens and, most important, the body follows the swing.

—BEN HOGAN

86 How to know how far you should hit each club

You may think you can hit your 5-iron 170 yards, but maybe you can really hit it only 160 with consistency. Here's a good way to find out how far you should hit each club: Take a 7-iron, for example,

full-swing instruction

and aim at a target 150 yards away and hit a dozen balls at it. Then, using the same club, hit a dozen more at a target 140 yards away. If your shots are grouped closer together at 140 yards, that's your best distance with that club. —BOB TOSKI

87 How to become a great driver

A few simple steps can make the difference between a passable drive and a great one. Try these things:

• Stand tall, with your upper body relaxed. Set your feet at shoulder-width and the butt of the club six inches from your belt buckle. Make sure your body is ready to respond, not tense or locked in place.

• Give yourself enough time to wind up as far as you can. Try to get your left shoulder behind the ball. Your weight should move in the same direction as the club.

• Swing smooth and accelerate. Staying in control will result in better contact—the biggest power key. Try to hold your finish until you see the ball land. —BUTCH HARMON

Short Game

Chipping, pitching, bunker play—these are the shots that separate Tiger Woods from the rank and file on the PGA Tour, and these are the shots that can turn a nineties-shooter into a golfer who breaks eighty regularly. Yet how many of us go to the driving range, hit a large bucket of balls into the void, and then go home? When it comes time to hit that forty-yard pitch shot onto an elevated green with water on three sides, do we have anyone to blame but ourselves when we can't get up and down?

88 How to hit every short-game shot solidly

On virtually every short-game shot, you want to start with your weight forward and keep it there. To get the proper feeling, put all of your weight on your left foot and move your right foot back so only the tip of your shoe is still on the ground. Hold the club in your left hand and balance yourself with it. Now simply turn your right hip back, keeping your shoulders and hips level. Stay on your left side as you turn through. You'll get a sensation of rotary action on top of a single axis, not a slide or a tilt. —STAN UTLEY

89 How to dial in your wedges

Spend some time on the range with your wedges, moving your hands down the grip in one-inch increments. By gripping down an inch, you can subtract five to eight yards without changing your swing. See how it affects your yardages. You'll have to get closer to the ball, but you'll still be making a full swing. —JUDY RANKIN

90 How to mirror your swing to improve wedge ploy

Just as with the full swing, the backswing on a wedge shot should mirror the follow-through. The club should stay on plane, and the clubface should stay square to the swing arc. The shaft should be on the same angle at the finish as it is at the top of the backswing. This brings consistency to trajectory and distance. —DAVID LEADBETTER

91 How to make a wedge back up

It's harder than it used to be to make a shot back up a ton. The old, wound balata balls spun more. Still, if you're determined to really spin one, use a wedge with extra loft and hit the ball with a descending blow. You've got to hit the ball first and then make the divot, so play the ball well back in your stance. Swing hard while staying in control. —PHIL MICKELSON

92 How to spin a half-wedge shot

If you want the ball to check and stop after a couple of bounces, or even spin back, you'll need a fair amount of clubhead speed. Think of the swing as striking a match. Make a short, aggressive swing with a compact finish. This helps produce the crisp contact needed to spin it and stop it. — DAVID LEADBETTER

93 Another way to spin your wedges

The good kind of spin—backspin—comes from hitting the ball cleanly, then making a divot after impact. The biggest mistake is trying to pinch down on the ball and rip out a big divot. This often leads to hitting the ground before the ball. To really put some stop on it, take one less club, so you're making a more aggressive swing. With a steep angle of attack, hit the ball while keeping your hands and wrists firm. Your divot should be a straight, shallow scrape at the target—not a worker's trench. Fight the impulse to play the ball back. Play it an inch in front of center with a short iron, so you can hit it higher. A high shot will come in more vertically and roll less, enhancing the effect of the backspin. — ERNIE ELS

94 How to hit the hated half-wedge

Many amateurs find the half-wedge—the thirty- to sixty-yard shot—awkward and, when sand or water is involved, downright scary. Try these tips to execute it well.

1. Address: Open your stance and play the ball slightly forward of center. Aim the clubface at the target.

2. Backswing: Cock your wrists fully and limit your arm swing.

3. Finish: Swing down and through, but at the end of your follow-through don't let the shaft get past parallel to the ground.

Thought: Be aggressive. I generate as much speed through impact as my restricted backswing will comfortably allow. —PHIL MICKELSON

1   2   3

short game

95 How to hit the lob shot

If you have little green to work with, you need to get the ball flying high so it lands softly and won't roll very far. To hit the lob:

1. Open your stance and play the ball off your left heel, with your hands just slightly ahead of the ball.

2. Swing back along your toe line.

3. Make a smooth backswing and accelerate down through the ball.

—JOSE MARIA OLAZABAL

96 How to hit an easier version of the flop shot

Some good players hit the flop shot from an open stance, with an open clubface. I use a different method that increases my margin for error. I stand farther from the ball and lower my hands—with a square clubface. This shallows out my swing plane and increases the effective loft of the club. Just like on the bunker shot, I keep my weight on my left side throughout the shot, and I bring the club around on a flatter arc, which gives me more margin for error. Even if I hit a little behind the ball, I'll still get a decent result.

—STAN UTLEY

97 How to hit a pitch shot over a bunker

This is a shot I see many amateurs having trouble with. It's no more difficult than one with a clear run-up to the flag. The biggest problem is distance control. To avoid the sand, amateurs tend to worry themselves into hitting the ball too hard. Don't agonize about that; take advantage of it. Focus on the far lip of the bunker rather than on the hole itself. Your inclination will be to hit the ball firmly, but not way past the flag. For me, a pitch shot means a relaxed posture and a stance that's a little open to encourage a slightly out-to-in swing shape. Then it's a smooth swing back, down, and through the ball. —SEVE BALLESTEROS

98 How to use one leg to hit better pitch shots

Hitting high, soft pitches close to the hole will save you strokes. You need to feel your hands and arms controlling the swing, the body stable and in support. Hit pitches with your sand wedge while standing on your left leg. Play the ball opposite your left foot. With a light and consistent grip pressure and soft arms, feel the resulting pendulum-like motion. This allows the weight of the clubhead to uncock the wrists at the appropriate time to consistently control the bottom of the arc (where the clubhead is at its lowest point in the swing). The result: solid contact and a high, soft shot. —JIM FLICK

short game

99   How to utilize a wedge's bounce

One of the keys to hitting good pitch shots is to let the clubface open properly during the backswing. The club always swings on an arc, and the clubface should be square to slightly open relative to that arc. The clubface should rotate open during the backswing—this gives you loft and lets you use the flange on the bottom of the club properly. The club will skid, instead of dig, when it hits the ground.

— HANK HANEY

100   How to hit a pitch shot from a downhill lie

A pitch from a downslope is relatively easy when you don't have any trouble in front of you. But when you need to carry the ball over something and hit it high, you have to be more precise. The primary goal is to stay stable over the shot, so you can make consistent contact. Swing your hands low and around your body, thereby increasing loft. Even though I'm trying to get the ball up, I haven't lifted the club high in the air to do it. The feel you want is of the club swinging down the angle of the slope. My only swing thought is to feel as if my hands are resting on my left hip at the finish. When you lift your hands out and away from you, you lift the club's leading edge into the ball. Bad move.

— STAN UTLEY

101 How to hit a short pitch

When you have a ten- to twenty-yard shot that requires some height, a chip won't do. Instead, try the short pitch.

1. Take a sixty-degree wedge to get the ball up quickly and easily.

2. Open your stance a little so your body is aligned left of the target.

3. Play the ball off your front foot's heel.

4. Hinge the club quickly on the backswing.

5. Swing down along your stance line, not the target line.

—DAVID TOMS

102 How to stop skulling and chunking chips

Here's a great drill to keep you from trying to scoop your chips into the air. Grip an iron about midshaft, so the butt end is pointing up and just outside your lead hip. As you take the club back, hinge your wrists slightly, so the butt end of the shaft doesn't hit your side. Now start your downswing by rotating your body toward the target, maintaining the wrist hinge. The goal is to avoid having the butt end of the club touch your body during the swing. If the club hits your side, it means that you let your wrists break down or you failed to make a body turn. —RICK SMITH

103 How to hit a great chip shot

Stan Thirsk has been my teacher and friend since I was a snot-nosed kid. The best advice I ever got from him was a chipping lesson when I was eleven. He taught me to open the face of a wedge, take it back outside the target line and up, then slice across the ball—hard. You can hit the ball more firmly this way. It will pop into the air, go a shorter distance, and land softly.

— TOM WATSON

104 How to chip to a pin in the back of the green

When the pin is all the way on the other side of the green, follow these keys to hit a better chip:

1. Choose the longest club that will let you land the ball on the green without running it past the hole.

2. Grip down an inch or two to control the club and improve your chances of solid contact.

3. Play the ball just behind the center of your stance, and put more weight on your front foot.

4. Turn your upper body through the shot on the downswing.

— ANNIKA SORENSTAM

short game

105 How to chip from sidehill lies

Most players have trouble when the ball is above or below their feet. From a sidehill lie, the ball will follow the direction of the slope and you have to allow for that. When the ball is below your feet, it will bounce and run to the right, so aim left. Stand slightly closer to the ball and set your weight left and more on your heels. Bend more at the waist, grip the club at its full length, and swing easier to adjust for the longer arc. When the ball is above your feet, it's going to go left, so aim right. Stand slightly farther from the ball and set your weight left but more on your toes to keep your balance. Grip down on the club and swing a little harder to make up for the shorter swing arc. — TOM WATSON

106 How to use a dowel to hit better chips

On a good chip shot, the hands lead the clubhead all the way through impact. You don't want to add loft by flipping your hands to help the ball into the air. Give yourself a visual to practice this. Stick a thin dowel into the hole on the butt end of your grip. Make some chip swings, but don't let the dowel hit your left side. If the dowel touches, the clubhead is beating the hands back to the ball. You are flipping. —CHUCK COOK

107 How the body should move in a chip shot

A lot of players get so fixated on the ball and on their fear of not making clean contact that they don't let the arms extend and the body rotate through impact. If your arms collapse and your body stops turning, your swing will bottom out behind the ball. That's how fat and thin chip shots happen. Feel that extension and body rotation through the shot, and turn your head and eyes to where you want the ball to land. That will help move the bottom of your swing forward, where it needs to be. — HANK HANEY

How to play golf with the President

It's easier to play golf with a President of the United States than it is with the great, big, important president of a great, big, important company that makes things nobody needs. I know this from experience, having played golf with both. You can joke with the President of the United States, especially if his name is George Herbert Walker Bush, Old 41. Well, up to a point. But you can't joke at all with the great, big, important president of a great, big, important company that makes things nobody needs. Make a joke with that guy, who is usually overclubbed and badly dressed, and he'll call in your banknotes, have your children kidnapped, and set fire to your house. Still, you need to be cautious when playing golf with the President of the United States. Here are five things it's best not to say:

1. "If the phone rings in that briefcase the guy over there is carrying, do you answer it before or after you three-putt?"

2. "Why do you want to give our ports away to the Democrats?"

3. "You meet a lot of celebrities. Is Alec Baldwin as short as Sean Penn and Barbra Streisand?"

4. "Have you ever paid a green fee?"

5. "I hate slow news days. Can we bomb somebody?"

— DAN JENKINS

108 How to set the wrists in the chip shot

On a basic chip, the tendency is to make a stiff, long backswing. I like to keep my weight forward and take a smaller backswing with more wrist cock. It really promotes a clean, downward strike on the ball. You're less likely to hit it fat or try to scoop it into the air.

— PHIL MICKELSON

109 How to chip onto a fast green

The basic fundamental in chipping to fast greens is to strike the ball with a downward clubhead movement. It gives you maximum control of the shot and creates backspin, which minimizes the chance that the ball will roll too far. To achieve this downward movement, play the ball back in your stance; keep your hands ahead of the clubhead until you are well into the follow-through; and accelerate the club into the ball just as you would on a putt. One of the best

short game

aids is to imagine how a ball would react if you tossed it by hand toward the cup. Roll the ball underhand, and then transfer this movement to the proper chip-shot technique. Judging a chip will soon become merely a matter of using your imagination.

— JACK BURKE

110 How to hit chip shots like a putt

Paul Runyan, who beat Sam Snead convincingly in the 36-hole final round of the 1938 PGA Championship, pioneered the concept of chipping like he putted. He didn't just use a putting grip, which helps minimize wrist action for more reliable contact; he also showed me how to set the club on its toe so the shaft is more vertical, similar to a putter's shaft. Take your normal putting grip, play the ball just inside your left heel, and tilt your body a bit toward the target, with the heel of the club off the ground. Keeping your body still, make a pendulum motion back and forward into the ball. — JIM FLICK

111 How to chip on an uphill lie

When playing a course with elevated greens, you'll frequently find yourself chipping on an uphill lie. For this shot, you need to sweep the ball off the slope. I recommend taking a less lofted club—the upslope will help get the ball into the air—and then making a swing that goes from low to high. In other words, the backswing should stay low to the ground, but the follow-through should move upward along the slope. Remember: when the ball lands, it will usually roll and not check up, so allow for that. — DAVID LEADBETTER

Yes   No

112 How to knock it close when you're in greenside rough

When you're just off the green and the ball is sitting down, you're facing the hardest shot in golf. Commitment is everything. You have to accelerate the club underneath the ball. For this shot I used my fifty-six-degree wedge. The key is swinging through until your hands are about hip high. Remember: don't baby it. You want to make sure your next shot is a putt. —NICK PRICE

113 An easier way to chip with consistency

On a chip shot, most pros hinge their wrists abruptly on the backswing to generate clubhead speed and create backspin. But I've found that my "dead-hands" approach, which uses very little wrist hinge, gives me more consistency. The ball doesn't stop as quickly, but I can always count on its behaving the same way. Plus, the swing is simpler and easier to repeat, so I recommend it to amateurs. At address, set your weight toward your left side and lean the shaft slightly forward (that's all the wrist hinge you'll need.) Then take the club back with your shoulders and forearms. All your hands do is hold on to the grip. The thought you want is to drag the clubhead through impact. Sometimes, when amateurs have too much wrist hinge, their impulse is to release the club on the way down and flick at the ball. With my style, the hands and wrists stay quiet.

—STEVE STRICKER

114 How to set up for an effortless bunker shot

Set up with a wide stance—your feet should be shoulder-width apart and your spine tilted slightly toward the target. Play the ball off your front heel and angle the shaft slightly away from the target. This gets the club's bounce working for you and increases the loft on the clubface. — STAN UTLEY

115 How to escape bunkers with hard, packed sand

Use your pitching wedge instead of the sand wedge. The flange of a sand wedge tends to bounce off the hardpan and into the ball and blade it. A pitching wedge will dig enough but won't bounce off the hardpan—and you can still play a traditional bunker shot. You won't get as much loft, but you can open the face a little to compensate. You should hit a little closer to the ball than normal, and use a V-shaped swing. A pitching wedge is also good from wet sand.

— TOM WATSON

short game

116 How to putt out of a bunker

If you aren't comfortable hitting a bunker shot, try the putt shot. It's especially useful from a bunker that doesn't have a high lip. As long as you can make crisp contact with the ball, you can make this shot work. But remember: if you ground the club, it's a two-stroke penalty. Getting the ball onto the green in one shot is the priority; leaving yourself with a makeable putt is a bonus. Practice this shot from a variety of situations, and I promise you that you'll have an easier time in the bunker and save yourself from making a big number. — SUZY WHALEY

117 How to hit sand shots like a sidearm pitcher

Not clear on the concept of hitting a bunker shot? Think of splashing the ball out of the sand as a motion similar to the way a baseball player throws a sidearm pitch. A right-handed pitcher starts by facing third base, the body perpendicular to the target, and finishes facing home plate, or square to the target. Meanwhile, the throwing arm moves across the body from outside the target to inside, continuing well past the point it releases the baseball. In a greenside bunker, the body rotates from the address position to a position square with the target as the club cuts across the target line from outside to inside. In other words, it's not an underhand toss or a scooping, tilting motion; it's much more of a rotational move, with the body staying in a level position. And the club releases through impact the same way the sidearm pitcher's arm continues to move after releasing the ball.   — RICK SMITH

118 How to play a bunker shot when the ball is sitting up

Don't be fooled by that inviting-looking situation in which the ball sits up on a clump of sand. It's one of the toughest trap shots. The tendency is to either "pick it clean" or take too much sand, meaning it comes out too soft (if at all). Play the ball a little right of center in your stance, and keep your weight on your front foot. Then swing the club as you would on a normal sand shot, but sweep down and through, not under and up.   — BILLY CASPER

short game

119　How to hit the dreaded fifty-yard bunker shot

I don't know about you, but I find it difficult to hit a sand wedge a long way out of a trap. If I were to try, I'd be swinging much too hard to have any sort of control. If the lip isn't too high, I normally play this shot with a 9-iron. It has the sharp edge you need to clip the ball away so that it will run up to the flag. First, open your stance—say about twenty degrees. Open the face of the club a little too. That will give the shot a slice flight, which is easier to control. Now make a three-quarter swing, contacting the sand and the ball together. You don't need a long follow-through. The success of the shot is determined by your backswing and by the quality of contact between the club and the ball.　　　　　—NICK FALDO

120 How to hit a long greenside bunker shot

When you are in the bunker but have to carry the entire bunker to reach the green, focus on your left hand, keeping the grip a little tighter than normal to make sure the clubhead doesn't turn over too much in the sand. If it does, you could end up hitting a low shot that flies into the lip.

As far as judging distance, you have to decide how big a swing to make. If you hit behind and under the ball, as you should, you can almost never make too big a swing. — JOHN DALY

121 How to regulate distance on bunker shots

Most amateurs have trouble gauging how far they will hit a sand shot. That's because they try to control with their backswings how far the ball goes. If the pin is close, they make a short, stabbing motion at the ball. Longer shots are marked by deceleration.

The key to distance control from bunkers is your follow-through. Let it dictate your yardage. For short shots, make a short follow-through; for longer shots, swing through to a fuller finish.

—COREY PAVIN

122 How to hit a higher shot from a bunker

For every sand shot, your clubface should be open at address, your body position should be open to the target, and your hands should be set lower than normal.

To play a higher shot than normal, use this technique: bend more from your knees, to lower your center of gravity, and drop your hands even lower. Tour pros can hit the ball almost straight up this way.

—HANK HANEY

123 How to play a downhill greenside bunker shot

Tilt your shoulders to conform to the slope and swing with the slope. You'll need to open your clubface considerably to the right in order to offset the decrease in the club's loft from swinging down the hill. Accentuate your open stance to the left to offset the open face to the right.

On this shot, many players try to lift the ball out and end up skulling it, so be sure to force the clubhead down and under the ball.

—CLAUDE HARMON

124 How to stop a ball quickly out of a bunker

When I'm faced with a bunker shot that I must hit high and stop quickly, I revert to a method advocated by Claude Harmon. At address, set the blade of your sand wedge open and place your hands on the club in a weak position (turned counterclockwise, or to the left). Play the ball forward, which puts your hands behind the clubhead. On the backswing, cock the club up quickly and fan it open by cupping your left wrist. From there, swing down into the sand behind the ball as hard as you want, releasing your hands fully. You want to feel that the clubhead is passing your hands through impact. You must do this or risk shanking the shot. Because you started from such an open clubface position at the top, the club won't dig into the sand. Instead, it will pass nicely under the ball and you'll get a high shot that always lands dead. —CURTIS STRANGE

125 How to get out when the ball is against the lip

Drop your left foot back and put all your weight on your back foot. While keeping your lower body still and hitting from your back foot, slam the clubhead into the sand directly behind the ball. You need to generate a lot of speed on the way down. For a short shot, use your most-lofted wedge. But for a longer greenside shot, go with a short iron to cover the extra distance.

—DEAN REINMUTH

short game

Putting

Instructors say that it's best to learn the game backward—meaning from green to tee. Putting accounts for roughly 40 percent of the strokes taken in any given round, but most amateurs devote little time to practicing it. It's a shame, because it's the quickest way to lower your score. For example, you could top your drive, skull your second shot, dribble your third onto the green, and then roll in a thirty-footer for par. Now, put that on the scorecard next to a par made by a golfer who hit a 300-yard drive, a 100-yard wedge shot, and two-putted. What's the difference? In golf, it's not how, it's how many.

Part of the problem with putting instruction is that there is no uniform way to putt. Some teachers say the shoulders should propel the stroke. Others say it's a wristy motion. Some players make a straight-back-and-straight-through stroke, while others make an arcing path. And we haven't even begun to contemplate putterhead shapes (mallets, blades), putter lengths (long, belly, standard), and putting grips. Putting seems like a simple concept—roll the ball into the hole—but much can be said about how to do it. Here is some of the best advice on the subject.

126 How to grip a putter properly

To let the putting action happen naturally, let the last knuckle of your left hand's middle finger rest in the lifeline of your right hand. The most common mistake people make is connecting that dot on the lifeline to the top of the left thumb. That forces your right forearm into a higher position relative to your left forearm, instead of the level position I like to see. —STAN UTLEY

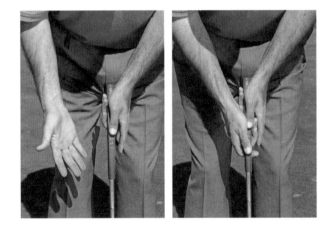

127 How to perfect your putting posture

If you haven't stood over a putt in a while, a quick refresher on posture will help. Whether you are using a belly putter or a conventional model, grip the club so the shaft is in line with your forearms and your forearms are parallel to the ground. Then simply bend over at the waist to sole the putterhead. The grip should run through the middle of your palms, not your fingers. This process will keep your forearms and the shaft swinging on the same plane, and help prevent flicking at the ball with a wristy motion.

—MARK WOOD

128 How to correct your posture when you putt

Standing taller gives me room to let the putter release instead of cutting across the ball. I had always played with a thirty-five-inch putter, but I found I was too hunched over and wasn't releasing the putter the way I should. I switched to a thirty-six-inch model and set up with the same bend at the hips, but my spine was no longer slumped. I immediately had more room to release the putter through impact, with the face rotating to the left. —ERNIE ELS

putting

85

129　How to roll your putts like a pro

To get the putterhead moving back correctly, hold your right elbow close to your side with your left hand and hit some putts. You'll start to feel a slight wrist hinge and forearm rotation in the backstroke—that's the putter moving back on plane. You'll also start feeling the most solid putts you've ever hit.

— STAN UTLEY

130　How to putt it straight back and straight through

During my prime, I tried to keep the putter square to the line of the putt throughout the stroke and did my best putting that way. If you want to try this method, I'd recommend lining up two clubs parallel on the ground, slightly wider apart than the putterhead. Practice hitting putts while keeping the putterhead from hitting or brushing against either of the shafts on the ground.　— TOM WATSON

131 How to ingrain a unified putting stroke

Place a club under your arms, and then hold it there as you grip your putter and set up to the ball. To get the ball to the hole with the club under your arms, you have to move your shoulders, arms, and putter as one unit—that's the key to building an effective stroke.

— RICK SMITH

132 How to use your left arm to hit solid putts

I feel that a firm-wristed stroke, with my arms swinging like a pendulum, is more consistent than a stroke that relies largely on wrist action. I try to swing the grip end of my putter back and forward so that my arms create the stroke. I try to accelerate my left hand and arm forward on all strokes so that my right hand doesn't take over and flip the putterhead upward or off line. — LEE TREVINO

putting

87

133 How to putt like a pool shark

It has been drummed into most golfers that they must concentrate on the ball when they putt. This isn't necessarily true—for instance, a pool player looks at his target and not at the cue ball. Experiments have shown that many golfers get better results by looking at the hole instead of at the ball. This causes them to stroke through the ball. Try a few practice putts this way. —DR. BERNARD NUNEZ

134 How to putt dead-armed

If you want to roll the ball better and make more putts, you've got to get tension out of your putting stroke. To understand what I mean, hold your right arm out and let a buddy support all of its weight. At first, I bet you have a hard time relaxing. But when you relax, have your buddy let go of your arm. It should drop straight to your side. That heavy-arm feeling is the same one you want as the putter is returning to the ball on your stroke. When you putt this way, it feels as if the putter is basically falling back into the ball after you get to the top of your backstroke. —STAN UTLEY

135 How to ensure you make a solid stroke

A good putter keeps the body still and the blade square by never allowing the left wrist to break down. The putterhead never passes the left hand. The putter is not picked up on the backstroke but is swung back low, although it should swing up naturally as the stroke gets longer. Remember: bend over far enough so your arms hang freely, with some flex at the elbows, and keep your eyes directly over the target line. —BYRON NELSON

136 How to get the wristiness out of a putting stroke

Many golfers prefer to putt with a "shoulder stroke." Their shoulder turn is the only movement used to accelerate the putterhead. They feel that this produces a more reliable stroke under pressure, largely because there is no independent hand or arm motion to open or close the putterface. I suggest that these golfers try spreading their hands and fingers to cover a larger area of the club's grip. This grip alteration will help eliminate all wrist action from the stroke.

—PEGGY KIRK BELL

137 How to putt sidesaddle

Back at the PGA Championship in 1966, I was leading after two rounds, but on the tenth green of the third day my hands jerked again in the middle of my stroke. I actually hit the ball twice in the same putt. The yips were back.

I decided then and there that I'd better come up with something or the twitches would finally end my career. On the next green, I set up to the putt like you'd do in croquet, straddling the line with the ball between my feet. I ran my right hand about halfway down the shaft. Then I moved the putterhead back and forward between my legs. The ball fell into the cup. Later, the USGA ruled it illegal to straddle the line, but I found a way to "sidestep" its decision. I simply moved my right foot to the left, setting up to the side of my putting line.

For senior golfers, or anyone having trouble with his or her nerves, the sidesaddle style might save the day. Here's how to do it.

1. Place your left hand on the grip as you'd grab a hand brake.

2. Put your right hand as far down the shaft as comfort will allow, with your index finger extended along the shaft.

3. Stand just to the left of your putting line.

4. Move the putter back like a pendulum.

5. Follow through with the left hand acting like a hinge.

—SAM SNEAD

138 How to make putting practice fun

Here are four games on the practice putting green that are fun and will improve your stroke.

1. The look-and-shoot game: Try to hole five putts before your partner does, the two of you putting at the same time. This gets you to react to the target.

2. The many-club game: Try to hit good putts with all kinds of clubs. This shows you that everything doesn't have to be perfect.

3. The nine-ball game: Hit nine putts in a row. Start loose, then try to put even less effort into each successive putt. This game will help you get more relaxed.

4. The use-your-instincts game: Try to make three putts from the same place but at different speeds. You have to trust your instincts. —BRAD FAXON

139 How to improve your lag putting

This cluster drill will help you lag better. First, hit a long putt across the practice green but not to any specific hole; pay attention to the pace of your stroke. Next, using that first ball as your target, stroke a putt with the same pace, trying to get the second ball close to the first ball. Then, on your next two putts, close your eyes and feel the stroke. With your eyes closed, guess whether the putt was short, long, or just right. Then open your eyes and hit one last putt. By now, you should have a heightened sensitivity for pace and distance.   — JIM MCLEAN

140 How to get the ball rolling straight

When I practice—and sometimes even when I'm on the course—I'll focus my eyes on a spot an inch or two in front of the ball along the target line, then just roll the ball over that spot. This helps keep my head steady and lets me get the ball started along the correct line.

— DAVE STOCKTON

141 How to turn knee-knockers into tap-ins

When Phil Mickelson practices, he'll line up ten balls in a circle, each one about three feet from the cup. He'll then work his way around the circle, putting every one of them into the hole. When he has accomplished that, he'll line up the ten balls again, sink them, and continue this drill until he has made a hundred in a row. If he misses, he'll often start over.

This drill will ingrain a confident stroke on short putts, and it also relieves pressure when you play. After Phil stands left or right of his putting line and makes practice strokes at the hole, the real putt is just one more stroke in succession. He's simply imagining he's back on the practice putting green, working his way around the circle of balls. —RICK SMITH

142 How to make more three-footers

When my short putting went sour a few years ago, my former caddie, the late Bruce Edwards, gave me a tip that helped: he suggested I look at my hands, instead of at the ball, as I take the putter back.

By doing this, you focus more on making a smooth stroke, and you won't get ball-bound—that is, trying to steer the ball into the hole.

Practice this before you take it on the course, but I promise it works. —TOM WATSON

143 How to drain the short ones

To make more short putts—the ones you should be making—set up square at address and control the stroke with your shoulders, not your hands. The butt end of the club should stay pointed at your midsection throughout the stroke.

To get a feel for this, try this drill: Set up with the ball just forward of center. Without making a backstroke, practice pushing the ball into the cup. Groove this feeling of extending the putterhead down the line.

Now step into your real putt with the right foot first, set the putterhead square to your putting line, and complete your stance. And keep those eyes down.

—ANNIKA SORENSTAM

144 How to improve your feel when you putt

The short game is all about touch and feel. That means your mind and hands must be in concert. To get a feel for long putts, try closing your eyes when you practice. Close your eyes when you practice short chips too.

Gaining consistency in these drills will help you gain confidence in your entire game.

—RENEE POWELL

145 What to practice when you want to lag it better

Instead of putting to holes on the practice green to learn how to lag the ball close to the hole, use this drill to get a feel for speed:

Grab a few balls and putt from one end of the green to the other, then turn around and putt back. You'll quickly get a handle on pace. As for technique, make a longer, slower backstroke, so you have generated some energy and some room to accelerate the putter.

—BUTCH HARMON

146 How to decide on the speed and break of a putt

When I help my pro-am partners read putts, I hear one question more than any other: "Which is more important, speed or break?" Both are, but you have to read the break correctly to have any chance of getting the speed right. Most amateurs under-read the break by 50 percent, so they end up subconsciously compensating for the bad read by hitting the putt harder to take some of the break out. When you miss a putt this way, the ball goes far past the hole, leaving you a lot of work coming back. Start by reading more break and trying to get a few putts to "die" into the hole. If you do miss, you'll have a tap-in left. —PHIL MICKELSON

147 How to make more putts by using your mind

The really important thing in putting is holding in your mind's eye a positive picture of the ball rolling toward the cup and dropping into the hole. When you hold such a picture in your mind, your subconscious will direct your muscles to move the putter in such a way as to "develop" the picture you are holding. If you think of three or four things while stroking the putt, you will find it impossible to hold this mental picture. —MICKEY WRIGHT

148 How to avoid three-putting

To avoid three-putting when you're faced with a long putt, pick a
spot three feet short of the hole and putt aggressively to that spot.
You'll rarely be short by more than three feet because you "charged"
to that short target. If you do hit the putt too hard, it can roll
five feet farther than your target, and you'll have only two feet
coming back. — JACK NICKLAUS

149 How to cure the yips

Tom Watson is one of the few tour players to overcome a full-scale
case of the yips. How did he do it? By going back to basics. Contrary
to some theories, the yips are not caused by opening or closing the
blade excessively, breaking down the left wrist, or anything else
mechanical. Those are outcomes of poor cadence. Putting should
be executed with a tempo of "one-two," and when that rhythm is
disrupted, mechanical flaws surface. When Tom found his rhythm,
he rediscovered his stroke. — JOHNNY MILLER

THE LIGHTER SIDE

How to tell a golf joke

It's all a matter of material, timing, and audience. You need to be topical. The
audience doesn't have to be composed of golfers, but it must understand the
nuances of a golf joke. In recent years, I've noticed a far greater grasp of golf
matters by my audiences. It used to be about 30 percent. Now I'd say 75.
My favorite foils are Gerald Ford and Tip O'Neill. In commenting on Gerald
Ford's renowned wildness off the tee: "There are nearly sixty golf courses in
the Palm Springs area, and Ford never knows which one he'll play until he hits
his first drive." Or "Alan Shepard found a golf ball on the moon. It had Gerald
Ford's name on it." — BOB HOPE

putting

150 How to putt on fast greens

There are two obvious points to remember when putting fast greens:

• Place your approach shot into a position that will not require a downhill putt.

• Avoid charging the hole with your putts. Get them to "die" into the cup.

But the real key to putting fast greens is the development of the delicate stroke. Positioning your hands very close to your body will give you a great deal of club control during the stroke. I even go so far as to anchor my left hand against my left leg on short putts, keeping it there throughout my stroke. —BILLY CASPER

151 More advice on how to putt on fast greens

I focus on two critical points when the greens are faster than normal: my grip pressure, and the pace or rhythm of my stroke.

1. Your hold on the putter must be light. If you are to control the pace of your putt, you must first control the pace at which the clubhead moves. A tight grip won't allow you to do that.

2. I focus on making my stroke as smooth as it can be. Put two tees in the ground about a foot apart. Next, place the ball midway between the two and take your stance. Now work on taking the club back to a point even with the first tee. Try that a few times until you can do it almost without thinking. Then hit some putts, making sure that your follow-through is a little longer than your backstroke. That's important. The follow-through has to be longer, because the putterhead has to accelerate through impact, even on a very fast putt. Vary the space between tees so that you get a feel for all lengths of putts. —PAYNE STEWART

152 How to coax a putt downhill

Hale Irwin is generally known for accurate driving and stellar iron play. But an often overlooked reason for his success is a great putting touch, especially on fast greens. Irwin is self-taught, and he discovered that on slick downhillers he should hold the putter more lightly than usual and allow the putterhead to pass his hands through impact. His left wrist actually cups a little on the follow-through. This motion increases the effective loft of the putter at impact by giving the feeling of adding backspin to the ball as it comes off the putterface. The result is a soft touch and a slow but true roll as the ball trickles down the slope. — JIM FLICK

153 How to sink a two-tier putt

On two-tier putts, particularly those that are uphill, it's all about distance control. You have to mentally flatten the slope. Think of the green as if it were a sheet that's bunched in the middle: if you pull it tight, it's a lot longer. The putt might look like twenty feet, but if you flatten the sheet (hill) it's twenty-two feet. Allow for that extra length.

— STEWART CINK

putting

154 How to make more short putts by using your left ear

Looking up too soon is the main reason golfers miss short putts. When you peek, your head moves, causing the putterface to open or close. Try aligning the putterface and then looking only at a point on the beginning of the target line. Keeping your eyes on that spot, hit the putt and listen for it to drop with your left ear. —BUTCH HARMON

155 How to hit breaking putts better

On right-to-left putts, Lew Worsham, the 1947 U.S. Open winner, used to recommend playing the ball slightly back in your stance. This encourages you to hit the putt more into the hill, with the face square to slightly open. It also promotes starting the ball on the high side of the line and allows you to make a firmer stroke. Likewise, do the opposite on left-to-right putts. Play the ball one ball-width forward. This ensures that you release the putterhead fully, so the ball starts slightly left of your line, instead of veering off to the low side of the hole. —JIM FLICK

156 How to improve your long putting

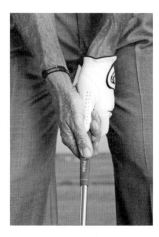

You need feel to roll a long putt close to the hole. This is not always easy to achieve, because of the way you ordinarily grip the putter. When you putt, the club, arms, and shoulders move in unison, and the hands and wrists stay passive. But this technique is more suited for short and medium-length putts, and you need some wrist action to create feel to hit long putts close to the hole.

Here's a tip I learned from a superb putter, David Frost. Take your normal putting stance, but switch to your full-swing grip. This will automatically give you the additional wrist action you need for long ones.　　　　　—DAVID LEADBETTER

Specialty/ Trouble Shots

Ben Hogan once said golfers should be judged by the quality of their worst shots, but I've often thought a better evaluation of ability is how well a golfer can get out of trouble. Whether it's a fried-egg lie in a bunker, a short pitch shot from deep grass, or a ball sitting in a divot hole, the best players can turn likely bogeys into impressive birdies.

For every nasty lie in golf, there is a way to extricate the ball. In this chapter, golf's magicians will let you in on their secrets for specialty shots, as will some of the game's top teachers.

157 How to cheat the wind off the tee

The driver stinger is a natural progression from my 2-iron stinger and just as effective in windy conditions. It's also great for tight fairways. I tee the ball a little lower than normal and play it toward the middle of my stance, which helps lower the trajectory. I flex my knees more than usual, which lowers my center of gravity and allows me to get on top of the ball at impact. I like to feel as though the emblem on my glove points to the ground through impact, and that after impact the clubhead extends straight down the target line to an abbreviated finish.   —TIGER WOODS

158 How to pick the ball clean from a fairway bunker

Three keys to hitting a solid shot from a fairway bunker:

1. Choose a club that will allow the ball to easily clear the bunker lip. Then grip down an inch or two and twist your feet into the sand for stability. Play the ball an inch behind your normal ball position.

2. The secret to hitting the ball flush is keeping your lower body quiet, so you don't lose your footing. To do this, I pinch in my knees at address. As you swing back, keep your weight centered and then shift smoothly into your downswing. Hit the ball first, then the sand.

3. Don't quit on the shot, as many amateurs do. Turn through to your left side and swing your hands up over your left shoulder. You want your right foot up on its toe at the finish and your belt buckle facing the target. —ANNIKA SORENSTAM

159 How to hit out of a buried lie in the bunker

It's not as hard as it looks. Set up with your spine tilted toward the target and your weight to the left. The ball position is forward, and your feet are spread more than two feet apart, to get your hands low and increase the effective loft of the club. Also set the clubface open. You need an extreme amount of wrist action. Your body should barely move as you chop down into the sand about an inch behind the ball. After impact, you'll feel like you're going to recoil. Do not try to scoop it out. Keep swinging. The ball will come out with a little higher trajectory. —STAN UTLEY

How to tell if you're not improving as a golfer

Not sure if you're getting any better at this game? Here are some signs you are *not:*

● Someone from the USGA's handicap department calls and asks how you're feeling.

● You're searching through the woods and find the ball you hit there . . . last Saturday.

● You go to your weekly lesson and find the instructor hanging from a shower rod.

● The guy who makes money by fetching balls from the water sends you a ham at Christmas.

● You ask for a bucket of balls and the guy at the range counter asks, "What for?"

● A cell phone goes off during your backswing and you hit your best shot of the day.

● Before you putt, you catch your partner writing down your score.

● You buy a dozen balls at the local golf shop and the salesman asks, "Should I put this on your tab?"

● Your forecaddie is wearing Kevlar.

● They create a new flight for you in the club championship.

—RON KASPRISKE

160 How to get out of a fried-egg lie

The sand wedge is a smart choice when your ball is sitting up nicely in the sand, but it's less effective when you have a buried "fried-egg" lie. A sand wedge comes equipped with bounce along the sole, which prevents the club from penetrating the sand deeply enough to slide under a half-buried ball. Because you want the clubhead to dig into the sand when the ball is buried, the pitching wedge, with its minimal bounce and sharp leading edge, is the better option.

specialty/trouble shots

Set up slightly open, and play the ball in the middle of your stance. Open the face of the pitching wedge, and aim at the rear portion of the fried egg. Break your wrists fairly quickly away from the ball. A short, upright backswing ensures that the clubhead approaches the ball on a steep angle. Make a sharp, knifing action through impact, and abbreviate your follow-through. The ball will roll some after landing, but will come out higher and land more softly than with the sand wedge. — PHIL MICKELSON

161 How to play a short bunker shot

On tour we talk about the danger of "short-siding" your approach shots— missing to the side of the green where the hole is closest to the edge. When you're short-sided in a greenside bunker, you have to pop the ball up quickly and stop it fast. To do this, I open the face of my sand wedge, lower my right shoulder slightly, and swing the club on an out-to-in path with plenty of force. I make more of a V-shaped swing than the usual U-shaped bunker swing.

Remember: you need clubhead speed to project the ball high and soft with spin.

— TOM WATSON

162 How to chip out of a bunker

Given a perfect lie (especially if it's a little uphill) and a shallow front bunker lip, it can pay to chip the ball rather than "explode" it. This means clipping the ball cleanly from the sand. Use a 7-iron, and play the ball no farther forward than the middle of your stance. Set your hands ahead of the clubface, and keep most of your weight on your forward foot. Your prime thought from then on should be: "Hands lead the clubhead through the ball."   —BILLY CASPER

163 How to play a ball that's in the bunker when you're not

Usually the ball will be lower than your feet. Tackle this situation by flexing your knees and "sitting down" to the shot more than normal. If the lip of the bunker is just forward of the ball, you'll need to raise the ball fast. So open the clubface at address, and keep it open—with the heel leading the toe through impact. But the essential thought here is to flex your knees and stay sitting.   —BILLY CASPER

164 How to get out of a fairway bunker using a hybrid

If you haven't found enough reasons to trade in your long irons for hybrids, here's one more: they're great out of fairway bunkers. A hybrid's longer shaft helps you make a sweeping swing, which is best in fairway bunkers, and the rounded sole cuts through the sand easier than an iron does, in case you catch the ball a little "fat." For stability, twist your feet an inch or two down into the sand. Grip down a matching amount to compensate. Play the ball back in your stance an inch or more than normal. Just before you start back, lift your chin. You'll find it easier to make your turn. Don't try to muscle the ball. Instead, take a club or two more and swing easy. And remember: thin is your friend in a fairway bunker.

—BUTCH HARMON

165 How to hit the ball close when it's under the lip

I call this my "pop shot." When I need to get the ball over a lip, I open the clubface and take a big backswing. Then I accelerate down through the ball but pull the club back before it hits the lip. It's like cracking a whip. It makes a pop sound and the ball floats right out. If I have a lot of distance to carry, I'll use anything up to a 5-iron to play this shot.

—DAVID TOMS

166 How to play out of a divot hole

When you are unlucky enough to find your ball in an old divot hole, don't waste time complaining. This shot is easier than you think. Play it the same way you would a bunker shot with your pitching wedge. Aim a little left of the flag and open the face of your club. Make a steep out-to-in backswing. The shaft should be just about vertical at the top. Then hit down about half an inch behind the ball. This will deaden the contact between the club and the ball, so hit it harder than you normally would for that distance. —SEVE BALLESTEROS

167 How to play short pitches from deep grass

When you are just off the green and have only a short distance to the hole and your ball is sitting down in deep grass, you should hit a shot that's actually closer to a bunker shot than to a pitch. You need to remember that thick grass will give you more resistance than sand, so you have to swing pretty hard. Open the clubface, grip down a couple of inches for control, and hit behind the ball, as you would for a bunker shot. The deep grass tends to turn the clubface closed, so hold the face open through impact. Accelerate through the shot and complete your finish. Don't just chop down into the grass. This shot won't spin at all, because you aren't actually hitting much of the ball. — ERNIE ELS

168 How to hit the ball flush from a downhill/sidehill lie

When the ball is on a slope, below your feet, pretend you're sitting on a bar stool and maintain that posture through impact. Widen your stance to improve your balance, and then flex your knees a little more than normal to get down to the ball. Take more club and swing easy, so you don't fall off the stool like a drunk! — JOSH ZANDER

169 How to hit a ball on a downhill lie

To hit a ball that's on a hill and below the level of your feet:

1. Stand à little closer to the ball than normal.

2. Make a more vertical backswing.

3. Maintain your address posture through impact.

— RICK SMITH

170 How to hit a ball out of deep rough

When the ball is down in the grass, use one club longer than normal, play the ball back an inch or two, and swing down on a steeper angle to catch the ball first. It also helps to aim slightly left and to open the clubface at address. You'll get more height on the shot, and the club will cut through the grass more easily.

— ERNIE ELS

171 How to putt from the rough

When you have only a few feet of rough between you and the green, use your putter, but play more of a chip shot. To play the fringe putt, take your putting stance, then let your left arm hang to your knee before taking your grip. This will lower your front shoulder, promoting a steeper backstroke that avoids the rough. Lowering the shoulder is particularly important if you're putting downhill. Let your wrists hinge going back and then stroke down and through. You'll feel more hit than you do on a putt. — BUTCH HARMON

SPECIALTY SHOTS

172 How to hit the ball low

Imagine a pane of glass that wraps around your body just below your shoulders. To hit a low shot, your club should go back and through below the pane of glass. The feeling is that you're swinging around your body. This shallow swing path will produce a lower, boring ball flight. — JOSH ZANDER

173 How to hit the ball superlow

I learned this trying to play under the wind in West Texas, where we have wind with a capital *W*. Move the ball back, but only slightly. Don't narrow your stance. Make it wider. You want the arc at the bottom of the swing to be shallow instead of steep, to send the ball out on a penetrating flight. Now just rotate your body; don't drive your legs. Swing easier and use more club. —RANDY SMITH

174 How to play a shot when your backswing is restricted

Tree branches sometimes force you to shorten your backswing. At address, open the clubface slightly. Then keep your knees bent and your lower body quiet to set up solid contact. When you swing back, your hands should go no higher than your waistline, and then accelerate down through the ball. —DEAN REINMUTH

175 How to play a shot when you don't have a clean lie or stance

With an object such as a rock interfering with your footing or swing path, take whatever stance will give you a solid base. Then make an armsy backswing with a bent left elbow and an armsy follow-through with a bent right elbow. Relaxed arms create speed, because you can't make much of a turn from this position. The ball will fly low and left, so aim accordingly.   —DEAN REINMUTH

176 How to hit a left-handed shot if you're right-handed

Occasionally you're prevented by a tree or fence from playing a shot right-handed. Some golfers will hit the ball with their back to the target, holding the club with only the right hand and chopping down on it. I prefer playing it left-handed, with the clubhead turned upside down. I use a fairly straight-faced club, like a 5-iron or 6-iron.

I choke down on the grip to reduce wrist action, and then all I try to do is make a long putting stroke. I concentrate on two things: striking the ball before the ground, and keeping my head down. Also, I make sure my grip is nice and light, so my arms can swing freely. Many golfers are scared of a left-handed shot, and they tighten their grip, which defeats them at the start.   —JERRY PATE

177 How to feather long irons

Fading, or feathering, a 2-iron is a shot of considerable value, but one often overlooked by many amateurs and also by some professionals. The typical 2-iron shot flies low and hot. The feathered 2-iron should start left of the target and move toward it. The flight should be high, and the ball should land softly. To hit it:

1. Weaken your grip, so that you can see only one knuckle of your left hand.

2. Aim to the left of the green.

3. Play the ball forward, with your hands over the ball.

—JIMMY DEMARET

178 How to play a knockdown shot

In golfing terms, the knockdown is a low-flying, highly controlled shot that bores through the air. Your setup is crucial for the knockdown. You need to make some adjustments from your normal address position. Play the ball farther back in your stance and put your weight more on your left side at address—about 70 percent. This encourages a downward blow. The knockdown requires a low follow-through and a slightly shorter swing. To hit the ball low, you must finish low.

Remember: the knockdown is not a punch shot. The biggest difference is that the knockdown goes the same distance as a regular shot but flies lower. At impact, I'm more aggressive with the knockdown. With the punch shot, I have a softer feeling.

—PAUL AZINGER

specialty/trouble shots

179 How to hit the ball under tree branches

When you find yourself off the fairway and in trouble behind a tree, you don't want to compound the mistake by hitting your next shot into the branches. If you use a club with too much loft, you have to not only punch it low but also take a much bigger swing. A big swing produces more backspin, which makes the shot go higher—the opposite of what you're trying to do. Instead, use a longer club. You can hit a lower, running shot with a normal swing, but a shorter backswing, which has less chance of getting caught up in trees or in the brush behind you.   —HANK HANEY

180 How to hit the ball over a tree

Picking the high route over an obstacle like a tree is a good move only when you're absolutely sure you can clear it. Otherwise, you're probably going to have the same shot all over again after the ball rattles off the branches. Move your ball position forward and set your weight a little more on your back foot. Open the clubface slightly to increase its loft and set your shoulders slightly open. Make an aggressive swing, because the more ball speed you create, the higher the ball will fly. This is a good shot to hit when you're a short iron's distance from your target. You lose backspin by hitting from rough, but the loft on this shot makes the ball land softly and settle fast.

—PHIL MICKELSON

181 How to hit a ball that's in the water

This thrilling and impressive shot can be successful only if your ball is in very shallow water and you're willing to soil your slacks. If more than one inch of water covers the top of the ball, you're in too deep and should drop out. The density of water will drag your club very sharply downward. The trick on this shot is to keep your weight on your left foot and drive the clubhead into the water immediately in back of the ball. The water will pull the club down quickly into the back of the ball, which will pop out. It works best with a pitching wedge and a maximum distance of thirty to forty yards. Don't use a sand wedge, because its bulging sole might bounce off the water.

—PAUL RUNYAN

182 How to chip the ball off soft ground like pine straw

If your ball is on a soft surface such as pine straw or leaves, don't ground the club, because the ball might move. Address it with the shaft more vertical than normal and the ball aligned with the toe (the heel should be off the ground). Hood the face slightly and aim right of your target. Keeping your weight on your front foot, take the club back more vertically, and don't release it through impact.   —RICK SMITH

183 How to chip off hardpan

You have to play the ball back in your stance. Set the heel of the club off the ground and the shaft perpendicular to the ground. To do this, stand closer to the ball. When you swing, keep the face square to your target and make a putting type of stroke by rocking your shoulders up and down. Focus on making contact with the ball first.

— JUSTIN LEONARD

184 How to get out of jail

My backswing is so long that I have a tough time whenever I have a shot near branches or anything else that interferes with the club. Here's my advice to anyone who wants to avoid tree branches during the backswing: grip way down on the club and make a shorter swing. Try to get hook spin on the ball by hitting down on it while releasing the club. Roll your right forearm over your left while extending the shaft toward the target through impact.   — JOHN DALY

185 How to hit a shot from the bunker's edge

You have to stand taller when the ball is above your feet like this. You still bend from the hips at address, just not as much. Feel as if you're raising your collarbone, which will give you room to swing the club around your body instead of chunking it into the ground before impact. To avoid hooking this shot, widen your stance by moving your left foot six inches toward the target. As you swing down, allow your head to slide slightly to your left, which will delay the release of the clubface.   —DEAN REINMUTH

Yes   No

Playing Strategy

Golf is often compared to chess because playing well often means thinking beyond the current shot. While most instructors and players would recommend clearing your head of swing mechanics when you play, the opposite holds true for playing strategy. You should never play golf without a plan. A simple question such as "What's the best way to play this hole to avoid a double bogey?" should be considered every time you step on a tee box.

But there's another side to playing strategy—one that's even more cerebral. Most experienced players will tell you that the real key to playing well is coping with emotions. Fear, nervousness, excitability, anger—any number of feelings can make a round of golf an exercise in mental control. In fact, the word *choke* is often linked to golf, but it's rarely spoken during a round because experienced golfers know what a bout of nerves can do to a golf swing. Rarely can you play well when you are bursting with emotion, and that goes for good feelings and bad.

This chapter is an attempt to get you to think your way through a round.

186 How to overcome first-tee jitters

The thing you need to remember about being nervous on the first tee is that you're not alone. That feeling of terror you're experiencing is something that we've all endured. My favorite is when you stand over the ball and your mind goes completely blank—you forget how to swing the club!

But I've got a secret way to overcome first-tee jitters: pretend you're Dean Martin. Dino was the Sultan of Smooth, the King of Cool. Nothing bothered him. Step to the tee and slip into Dino mode—I don't mean get drunk. Dean knew better. "If you drink, don't drive," he once said. "Don't even putt."

—GARY MCCORD

187 How not to choke

When I feel myself tightening up under pressure, I shake my hands at the wrists like a swimmer who's on his mark ready to start a race. Another tip: Visualize your swing in slow motion. In fact, slow down everything you do and you will probably be going at about normal speed. Breathing exercises are also good. Take deep breaths. Also, concentrate on gripping the club lightly. Grip the club just firmly enough to control it. —TOM WATSON

188 How to overcome your fear of the water

When amateurs tell me they have a problem hitting over water, I tell them to take some balls one evening and practice hitting shots over the water until they do it successfully a lot. I tell them to look at it as a challenge and visualize keeping the ball dry until the water doesn't exist in their mind.

There's one hole the pros really fear, and it's not the seventeenth at Sawgrass. It's the fifteenth at Augusta National. They're usually standing on a downhill slope looking at water in front of the green and behind it. It requires a precise shot. If they hit the ball long or fat with a longer club, or spin it too much with a wedge, they'll end up wet.   —BOB ROTELLA

189 How to overcome nervousness

A big factor in competing successfully is the ability to control nervous tension. Sooner or later, the jitters hit every golfer, from Ben Hogan on down. They are nothing to be ashamed of. Positive thinking can help you overcome such tension. When I feel nervous, I simply direct my thinking toward making a good shot. I visualize how a good shot will feel and look. Then I give it the best swing I can.   —GARY PLAYER

190 How to improve your chances of playing better

Golf is a game of finesse, rhythm, and flow. Mentally, it's a game of cool and calm. People who have a temper on the course make golf way too important. You don't see a lot of great players getting mad on the days they perform well. Staying calm is crucial. You need to know how to motivate yourself the right way. —BOB ROTELLA

191 Why you should waggle

The main goal of waggling is to preview a takeaway in which the clubface stays square to the arc of your swing—not square to the target. That's a hard thing for many players to visualize, because they're so focused on putting the club in the right position at impact. Get this takeaway move right with your waggle and the club will come back to impact in good position automatically.

—HANK HANEY

192   How to stay focused

Golfers often say they are distracted by players in their peripheral vision, by a car alarm going off in the distance, or by someone casting a shadow over their ball. In fact, most of the time these players are worrying about hitting a bad shot instead of focusing on the target and their pre-shot routine.

Distractions are part of the game. Golfers who accept this and view them as a challenge aren't as bothered by them. One way to become mentally tougher is to expose yourself to distractions, so they don't bother you. Every now and then, ask your friends to talk, rattle pocket change, or move around while you putt or hit shots. Soon you won't even know they're there.   —BOB ROTELLA

193   How to beat the eighteenth-hole jitters

One of the worst words in sports is *choke.* If your match has come down to the final hole, sports psychologist Gio Valiante has some advice. Valiante has worked with many tour pros, including Chris DiMarco, Justin Leonard, and Davis Love III. Gio's tips:

Accept fear: "All the pro golfers I work with know that nervousness and fear will happen. The first step in dealing with the jitters is to accept them and learn to hit the ball while you have them."

Stick to a routine: "It helps get a golfer's mind on hitting the best shot possible, and it buffers against fluctuations in emotion."

Focus on targets: "What is my strategy for this hole? How do I want to hit this shot? What's my target? These questions keep your mind on the task and not on failure."

Lighten your grip pressure: "When fear strikes and anxiety levels spike, capillaries in the hands constrict and muscles in the hands and forearms tense up. These effects tighten your grip, preventing the proper setting and release of the club. By lightening grip pressure, a golfer can combat the physiological effects of fear." —RON KASPRISKE

How to live with second place

There is a widely held belief among golfers who finish second in tournaments that they are the tragic victims of Billy Bob Destiny or Joe Tom Fate, those culprits who seem to know how to cast evil spells over a man's putting stroke, if not his tee ball as well. As someone who has spent a lifetime finishing second in my own meager circles of competition, I can speak with some authority on the subject. Without any doubt, it is God's work. You simply have to learn to live with it and understand the following rules:

1. If your car starts in cold weather, you'll finish second.

2. If your household air-conditioning works in hot weather, you'll finish second.

3. If all your children are employed and live in their own homes, you'll finish second, or worse.

You can't have it all. But you can gain new respect for the golfer who finishes second, the downtrodden runner-up, if you take a little trip with the immortals through the history of major championships. It's a silver mine. Consider Jack Nicklaus. Everybody on this side of the Balkans is aware that Jack owns twenty major championships, but it is often overlooked that he has been a runner-up in nineteen. —DAN JENKINS

194 How to make a pressure putt

If you do feel some tension creeping in before you hit a putt, it's best
that you admit it to yourself and do something about it. I find it
helpful to ball my hands into fists, then spread my fingers very wide,
extending them as far as I can. I'll also make a point of standing a
little bit taller when addressing the putt, because I feel this allows
me to make a freer stroke.   —DAVE STOCKTON

195 How to overcome nerves and sink an important putt

When David Duval made a six-footer to
shoot fifty-nine at the 1999 Bob Hope
Chrysler Classic, he told me he didn't
even read the putt: "I just got over
it, saw it, and putted it. I trusted my
instincts." Chris DiMarco also trusted
his instincts when he sank the winning
putt at the 2005 Presidents Cup. You
should do the same. See yourself making
the putt. Trust your instincts and have
the attitude that you don't care whether
it goes in.   —BOB ROTELLA

196 How to plan your strategy on any hole

No matter whether the hole is a par 3, par 4, or par 5, you should plan your attack from the hole back to the tee. Start by knowing where the flag is. That will determine how you play the hole. For example, if the flag is tucked into the left side of the green behind a bunker, with plenty of green to the right, the best way to approach it is from the right. In that case, stand on the left side of the tee box so you'll be hitting toward the right side of the fairway or green. Planning the hole from the cup back to the tee gives you the best position for every shot. —HALE IRWIN

197 How to speed up your round

EDITOR'S NOTE: *In the 2006 Verizon Heritage, PGA Tour pro Ryuji Imada played in an hour and fifty-one minutes, and shot a two-under-par 69. Here are his tips for playing faster:*

- Have a few clubs out before you get to the ball.
- Take one practice swing, then hit it.
- Have your caddie walk ahead of you on tee shots. No caddie? Keep your eye on the ball until it lands.
- Don't mark short putts.
- Get your yardage as you walk or ride up the fairway.

—RON KASPRISKE

198 How to be a better weekend golfer

You don't have the kind of time tour pros do to devote to practice, so you need every handy tip you can get when it's time to play your one round a week—or month. Here are several of my favorites to save you a few strokes:

• Take one more club than you think you need to reach the green.

• Keep your head still while putting.

• In the left hand of your grip, you should see only the thumb and two or three knuckles.

• Don't be too anxious. Complete your backswing before starting your downswing.

• Transfer your weight during the swing by turning, not by swaying.

• Use lighter clubs.

• Don't "hit from the top." Distance comes from a delayed uncocking of the wrists.

• Swing a club at least once during the week.

• Always hit some practice shots before going on the course.

• Chip with a less lofted club.   —GARY PLAYER

199 How to stop the bleeding

Perhaps one of the hardest things in golf is coming back from a poor start to a round or a bad run of holes. But there are things you can try on the course, things that can make a potentially disastrous round at least mediocre.

Here are some tricks I've picked up over the years:

• Make fast practice swings with your wedge: Most amateurs let their driver swing them, rather than vice versa. If you start missing fairways, make fast practice swings with your wedge. You want a feeling of control. After a few swings, get up to the next tee and reproduce the feeling of control you had with the wedge.

• Practice some swings in heavy rough: It's easy to start steering shots. You need some aggression to get rid of that tentative feeling that comes from steering the ball. Find a patch of thick rough and swing an iron through it a full speed. Commit to this type of rip and reproduce it with your next shot.

• Two practice swings, then go: Get your rhythm and natural athleticism back by making two practice swings. Try to emulate the shot you're about to hit, take one last look at your target, and then go!

• Putt along the shaft: while you're waiting to putt, lay a club on the ground and trace your putterhead along its shaft line to get your stroke back.   —NICK FALDO

200   How to survive when your game is leaking oil

To me, golf is a game in the air and also a game on the ground. People always forget the second part. When you're not hitting it well, try to keep the ball on the ground as much as possible. It's easier to manage your game and stay out of trouble. But don't steer it. The golf swing is all about motion. Amateur golfers often try to steer the ball to the target instead of making a rhythmic, flowing swing. When you're hitting it poorly, focus on finishing your swing.

—NICK PRICE

201 How high to tee the ball on par 3s

EDITOR'S NOTE: *Amateurs often struggle with how high to tee a ball when using an iron. You still want to hit this shot with a descending blow, and Jack Nicklaus has the perfect formula:*

On par 3s, tee the ball just high enough so the bottom of the ball is above the top of the grass. —JACK NICKLAUS

202 How to score better on par 5s

When you get to the tee on a long par 5, I know you want to let the shaft out on the driver and try to bomb it down there. But a big tee shot is not always the best strategy. What you want to do is put yourself in a position to hit your favorite shot into the green. So if that's a 120-yard shot and the par 5 is 500 yards, then a 200-yard tee shot and a 180-yard second shot will do the trick. —ERNIE ELS

203 How to hit a tight fairway with your driver

Some fairways are so narrow that they look like bowling alleys. So to keep it in play off the tee, start by teeing the ball lower. Then hit it with your normal swing, not a steep punch swing. You'll get a lower trajectory and more roll—almost like topspin—instead of the sidespin and curve you might get on a higher shot.   —CHUCK COOK

204 How to stay (relatively) dry in the rain

I grew up in Oregon, where if you didn't play in the rain you didn't play much golf. In the rain, your paramount concern is to keep your hands and grips dry. Towels, umbrellas, keeping your hands in your pockets between shots, and walking with your palms down—these are all musts on a wet day. Also watch for water seeping up into your bag from the bottom, which is where your grips are.

—PETER JACOBSEN

205 How to play golf in wet weather

Every shot you hit on a rainy day is likely to be different. How the rain will change your strategy depends partially upon how long the water has been spilling onto the course. These are your problems and how to cope with them:
• Play the ball back in your stance to ensure ball-first contact.

• Pitch to the hole. A chip and run-up are inadvisable on a wet day because it's difficult to judge how much casual water is on the green.

• Putt or chip from sand traps. A sand wedge will bounce off the wet sand. —BYRON NELSON

206 How to gauge distance when you grip down

The knockdown is great for approach shots. You might normally hit a 7-iron 150 yards, but you'll be more accurate if you learn to hit a 5-iron 150 yards. All you need to do is grip down an inch. Think "one inch = two clubs."

—JOSH ZANDER

207 How to play to an elevated green

Few golfers enjoy playing to elevated greens. The flag is hidden, the distance is difficult to judge, and players are goaded into trying to hit the ball higher than they normally do.

The key is to know that this is a yellow-light shot and requires caution, not a green-light shot you attack aggressively. Take at least one extra club. Don't try to hit the ball high by positioning it forward in your stance—this is especially dangerous when the flagstick is up front. Don't try to hook the ball, because a draw flies lower than a fade and you'll go over the green. Just make your normal swing and try to get the ball on the green, as opposed to hitting it stiff. When you climb the hill to see where the heck your ball wound up, accept the outcome and move on.

— JOHNNY MILLER

208 How to drive a dogleg hole

Of course you're going to cut off the dogleg. The fairway might be right in front of you, but the green is over there. If you have to take it over the trees or carry some distant obstacle, you need to hit your drive high and far. My advice is to use the longest tees you can find (four inches is the longest the rules allow). You also need to increase your launch angle: tee the ball off the outside of your left foot, tilt your shoulders so the left one is higher than the right, and put 60 percent of your weight on the right foot. Imagine a pterodactyl hovering over the spot on the dogleg you want to carry and try to knock it out of the sky. Hey, it's extinct anyway. — JOSH ZANDER

209 Another approach to dogleg holes

Understand your strengths and weaknesses and apply them to specific situations. Are you aggressive or conservative by nature? Is there a prevalent shape to your shots?

On a dogleg, it's tempting—and often risky—to cut the corner and shorten the hole. Instead, take advantage of your natural tendencies. If you slice, you should be aggressive on doglegs to the right. If you hook, be aggressive on left doglegs. If the wind is helping you, so much the better. When the doglegs go in the direction opposite your typical shot, be conservative. — TOM WATSON

How to tell that it's too cold to play golf

Not sure if it's too cold to play today? Some warning signs:
- *Every* tee time is available.
- You try to spit on your clubface and it freezes, in midair.
- The starter's name is Burl Ives.
- You call the pro for a tee time and he answers—in Barbados.
- You develop the yips from shivering.
- Your Eskimo friend cancels, saying he forgot a dentist appointment.
- You can putt out of a water hazard.
- Instead of carts, the course uses dogsleds.
- The cart girl pulls up on a snowmobile.
- You open the door to the starter shack and the guy's in there ice fishing.
- The super's dog is chasing penguins off the course.
- You discover hand warmers are good just about anywhere you put them.

—RON KASPRISKE

210 How to beat the par 3s

The term *one-shotter* applied to par-3 holes is the greatest misnomer in golf since a California rules chairman tabbed the Pacific Ocean as "casual water." A par 3 can produce a six or even a seven on your scorecard. Here is some advice to help you avoid big numbers, especially when you miss the green:

- Use one club longer to an elevated green.
- Don't try to squeeze more distance from your shot than backswing space permits.
- Test the rough with a practice swing to determine how much resistance it will offer your swing.

playing strategy

135

• Set your wrists faster on the backswing when you're playing out of the rough.

• Often it's smarter to putt the ball when you have a downhill lie close to the green.

• Be sure that on a short, uphill chip you make the clubhead follow the slope down on the backswing and up on the finish.

—BYRON NELSON

211 How to play to a par 3 over water

On a long par 3 over water, you can fire at the flag and try to birdie the hole. But realistically, what are your chances of pulling this off? Instead of trying to make a two, you should be more concerned with avoiding a five. If you're a 100-shooter, your target should be as far from the water as you can get, even if that area is just off the green. If you're a ninety-shooter, you should play for the fattest, safest part of the green. If you break ninety or even eighty, you can play closer to the flag, but only if you're hitting it well that day.   —NICK PRICE

212 How to score on an uphill par 3

I remember a great comment Johnny Miller made about the eleventh hole at Shinnecock Hills during a U.S. Open. He said that on an uphill par 3 people tend to miss to the right because they hang back on their right side in an effort to hit the ball higher.

The solution is to keep the shoulders more level at impact by making sure you transfer your weight to your left side on the downswing the same way you would on a normal shot. The clubface will square up for better contact and accuracy. Your weight should go mainly to your right heel at the top of the swing and to your left heel at impact.

— TOM WATSON

213 How to hit the fairway when you need to

When you're trying to finish off a round, you should be more concerned with accuracy than with distance off the tee. One way to ensure this is to tee the ball low, with the top of the ball just above the top of the clubhead. Even better, if you're a good player, is to kick up a little mound of turf and hit the ball from the grass. Either method encourages you to hit the ball lower on the clubface, thereby reducing sidespin.

— KEN VENTURI

playing strategy

214 How to handle a "flyer" lie

Your lie influences your club selection, how you set up to the ball, and the kind of shot you play. Pay special attention when your ball is partially buried in the grass. We call this a "flyer" lie because grass will get in between the clubface and the ball at impact. As a result, the ball will have less backspin and generally fly farther and roll more than a normal shot. There are two ways to play a shot from a flyer lie.

• Choose a club that is one less than normal.

• Aim slightly left, open the clubface a bit, and stand a little closer to the ball. —TOM WATSON

215 How to drive into the wind

To succeed on drives into the wind, play the ball a bit farther back in your stance than normal and concentrate on striking the ball as squarely as possible.

Playing the ball an inch or so farther back will enable you to make contact when the clubhead is neither descending nor starting upward. This will give you a lower shot and produce less backspin.

To strike the ball as squarely as possible, keep your head in a steady position throughout the swing. Focus your attention on the back of the ball and swing at your normal tempo.

—CARY MIDDLECOFF

216 How to improve your accuracy off the tee

When you're getting ready to tee off, focus on where you want the ball to go—and don't be vague about it. Shrink your target zone to something precise and clear your mind of everything else. One of the best images I use is a ring of fire, like the ones those dolphins leap through at SeaWorld. First, pick a precise spot where you want your ball to land, and then imagine a flaming ring ten to twenty yards in front of you on that target line. All you should be thinking about is threading that ring with your tee shot. —JIM MCLEAN

217 What to do if you're in between clubs

If you're in between clubs, take the longer club, choke down a little, and make an aggressive swing. That's better than not choking down and swinging easier, which may cause you to decelerate.

—JACK NICKLAUS

218 How to play the wind

On a really windy day, change your target rather than trying to fade or draw the ball into a crosswind. Downwind, run the ball onto the green; into the wind, pitch it. Leave your swing alone in the wind. Make changes only in ball position and clubface position to outsmart the breeze. —BYRON NELSON

playing strategy

219 How to look smart when you lay up

Always make a firm decision about the yardage you want for your next shot. Don't just chip out of trouble or blindly hit the longest club you have down the fairway. Be aggressive enough to make your next shot easier. Also, you need to concentrate on this shot just as much as on any tee shot or approach. Don't take it for granted.

—DAVID TOMS

220 How to hit a fairway off the tee when you really need to

Set up by the left tee marker, tee the ball high, and aim down the left edge of the fairway. Catch the ball on the upswing and swing to a nice, high finish. This easy-to-repeat swing will start the ball left and fade it to the middle.

—DEAN REINMUTH

221　When to attack the pin

Next time you're about to hit an approach, run through this
checklist, and go for the flag only if you answer yes to every question.
If not, play for the fat part of the green.

• Is your lie good?

• Would you hit the green at least seven out of ten times from this
yardage?

• Does the hole location match your shot shape (e.g., a fader will
have a hard time with a pin tucked left)?

• If you miss the green, are you likely to make no worse than
bogey?　　　　　　　　　　　　　　　　　　　　　　—NICK PRICE

222　How to hold a hard and fast green

When greens are hard and fast, don't aim
at the pin. Concentrate on just getting
the ball onto the green and keeping it
there. When it comes to holding a hard
green, a lot depends on how hard you
swing. If you're strong, play the ball
farther back in your stance and make
a steeper downswing. That should put
enough spin on the ball to hold the green,
especially if you aim for the center. If you
don't swing hard, take one club longer
than normal and try hitting a higher
shot. To do that, you want to play the
ball farther forward in your stance and keep your body behind the ball
through impact. Play to the front.　　　　　　　—MARK O'MEARA

223 How to read a green with your feet

When reading putts, many people focus their attention near the hole. However, don't neglect the area around the ball. It will affect the putt's initial break, a key factor in determining the putt's direction. This is information you can take in not only with your eyes but also with your feet. After looking at the putt, confirm your read by feeling for the slope of the ground around the ball as you're taking practice strokes. It will help you start the ball on the correct line.　—JUSTIN LEONARD

224 How to putt on wet greens

When selecting your line on a wet green, keep in mind that moisture will prevent the ball from breaking as much as it would in dry weather. Also, on slow, wet greens, you can afford to strike the ball firmly for the back of the cup without fear of rolling it far past. This firm stroke also requires that you play less break.　—TONY LEMA

225 How to get off to a good start in any match

I recommend that you play the percentage shot at the beginning of a match and not take any unnecessary risks on the early holes. Keep the ball in the fairway and get it on the green. By keeping the ball in play, you're forcing your opponent to do the same or fall behind in a hurry.

Or let's say you've driven into the rough and your opponent is in a fairway bunker. You know he can't get to the green from there, so don't gamble on a spectacular shot to the pin. Just try to get your ball out somewhere near the green where you'll have the advantage on the next shot.

Get the momentum going in your favor. Before you know it, your opponent will be putting so much pressure on himself that he'll be in trouble.　　　　　　　　　　　　　—HALE IRWIN

THE LIGHTER SIDE

How to throw a club

First of all, Ol' Tom never threw clubs. It was just that in the old days the grips would get slick, don't you see?

I always thought Arnold Palmer was the worst club thrower I ever saw. He would hit a bad shot and then throw the club backward. Finally, I had to take him aside and tell him that if he was going to throw clubs he should throw them in front of him. That way you can pick them up on the way to the green.

—TOMMY BOLT

226 When to make someone putt out

Putting, more than any other part of the game, is played in the mind. Try to get your opponent thinking on the greens.

In a match, pay close attention to his general demeanor as he approaches and strokes his first short putt. It's easy to tell if he is confident or not. If he looks a little unsure, make him hole every short putt. Nine times out of ten, he will miss one sooner or later. And, more to the point, he will know that you know he is a little edgy.

If, however, your opponent holes out well, give him a few short ones—but not all of them. After a while, make him putt one. With luck, that will make him think, "Why is he making me putt? Can he see something I can't?" Sometimes that is enough to win a match.

—SEVE BALLESTEROS

227 How to control your opponent

You can control a match by controlling your opponent's play. Here's how:

• Take charge on the first tee. Show him the ball you're playing, offer to keep the card, ask him the order of play. Show him who's boss.

• Make him putt out. Nothing irks a weekend golfer more than having to putt two-footers.

• Control the pace, but play at your usual speed.

—PETER MORRICE

228 How to knock out your opponent

You might like the person you're playing a match against, but a good rule to remember is show no mercy. If you can win ten-and-eight, go for it. Here are some ideas on how to win convincingly:

- Approach each round with a fresh mind.
- Make every shot the critical one. Forget about the last one, and don't worry about the next one.
- Consider difficult conditions an advantage. Good players love bad weather.
- Keep moving forward. If I can win six-up instead of five, so be it.
- Always give yourself more than one way to play a shot, and go with the percentages when determining which is the best to hit.
- Practice your weaknesses before you play.
- Use your warm-up for tempo.
- Keep your emotions on an even keel.
- When indecision creeps in, start the process over. — HALE IRWIN

229 How to rattle your opponent the right way

Try these tactics to distract your opponent:

- Make your opponent putt the first two-footer he sees. This establishes that you, not he, are in control of his golf ball and that nothing will come easily.
- If his par attempt rolls three feet past the hole and you're looking at a fifteen-footer for birdie, don't give him the putt right away, if at all. The last thing you want to do is find yourself worrying about making a par putt that, if missed, would result in a demoralizing half.
- If your opponent is a fast player, you might want to move a little slower to upset his rhythm. — JOHN HAWKINS

How to know when to press

You can cut your losses, and even make a buck or two, by calling for a press in a Nassau or other match-play wager. Here's when you should do it:

• Most presses begin when a side is two down, and serious players often make them automatic. Clarify this on the first tee.

• Agree in advance whether the recipient of a press can decline it.

• It's wise to begin a press on a hole where you're receiving a handicap stroke. If you're giving shots, don't press.

• If you're the better player, press on par 3s, where you'll likely be playing your opponent straight up, because par 3s are usually high-handicap holes.

• If you're playing a four-ball (better ball) match, consult with your partner before pressing. He has as much on the line as you.

• When trailing late in a Nassau but playing fairly well, suggest a press for the eighteen-hole match at the same time you press the nine-hole bet. It doesn't hurt to ask, and if accepted this double bet could intimidate your opponent and swing the momentum your way.

• Consider upping the ante on a specific press. If you're down two three-dollar press bets on the back nine and are feeling frisky, suggest that the next press be worth five dollars. Everything is negotiable.

—GUY YOCOM

231 How to win a match against your golf buddy

You play the same guy every week and it has been fairly even up to this point? If you want to finally take control of your weekend battles, follow this advice:

• Dig it out of the rough: To stay in any match, you have to be able to recover from crooked shots. For deep rough shots, feel like you're driving the heel of the club into the grass right behind the ball.

- Go deep: If you have a lower handicap than your opponent, take him all the way to the back tees. Most mid- to high-handicappers struggle with long tee shots and forty-yard pitches. Those are what you'll see a lot of from the back tees.
- Work the numbers: The real match-play assassins play safe when they get a stroke. Fairways and greens. A boring par/net birdie is tough to beat.
- Safe, not weak: If your opponent is in trouble, play it safe. But don't fall into a common playing-conservative trap. Make a positive, assertive swing with that 3-wood. Don't steer the ball, or you'll end up in just as much trouble.
- Give and take: Make him putt if there's a decent chance he could miss—say, something outside three feet.
- Money matters: If you have to get your checkbook out to pay off at the end of the round, you're playing for too much money and the stress will show in your game. —RANDY SMITH

232 How to read (and wreck) your opponent

I learned this valuable secret on reading an opponent in 1936 from a little pepper pot named Freddie Martin, who was the manager of golf at the Greenbrier hotel. "Matches can be won," he used to tell me, "when you're not even holding a stick. Man still is a primitive being. Let someone betray a weakness and he's ready for the kill."

• Watch their eyes. Fear shows up when there is an enlargement of the pupils. Big pupils lead to big scores.

• Take a good look at your opponent's lips on the first tee, and then check throughout the round. If he gets white around the lips, his nervous system is acting up.

• If your opponent starts to scratch or act like his clothes are uncomfortable, it's nerves too.

• When your opponent takes two waggles, then suddenly switches to three or four, he's hurting inside.

• Notice the natural rhythm of your opponent's stride. When he starts to speed up and charge toward the ball, the poor guy is losing his cool.

Even Ben Hogan, great as he was at hiding his emotions, slipped once. I was playing Ben in the old match-play tournament at San Francisco and I had pulled even on the sixteenth hole. We were walking down the seventeenth fairway and Byron Nelson pointed out to me that Hogan was talking with the crowd. Now, that's something Ben never did—talk to people when he played. I thought, "Ben, it looks like I've got you today." Sure enough, on the eighteenth Ben overshot the green, and I won with a par.

—SAM SNEAD

233 A few more tips on how to win your next match

There are some things about match play that never change from one opponent to the next. Remember these commandments:

• Concentrate on the probable state of your opponent's mental condition. It lessens the tension within yourself.

• You should play the golf course and not the man, unless your opponent has the honor and hits a shot out of bounds or in an obviously unplayable situation. You should use sound judgment by playing for a sure winning bogey or par.

• The first hole is just as important as the last one.

• Never take your opponent lightly.

• Never go into a match thinking your chances of winning are less than fifty-fifty.

• Never give up. —PAUL RUNYAN

Rules and Etiquette

It's probably tempting to skip this entire chapter. After all, the rules of golf are more complicated than trigonometry, and etiquette . . . ? Please. No one wants to be told how to hold a salad fork, let alone where to stand while someone else is putting. However, knowing the rules and etiquette of the game will not only lower your scores but help you play faster and improve your chances of being invited back to that great country club.

No one can expect you to know even half of what's in the *Decisions on the Rules of Golf* (the official rule book, which is more than 500 pages long). However, there are many rules that you should know forward and backward, such as the difference between a red-staked hazard and a yellow-staked one. The same goes for etiquette. If you don't know to be quiet when someone else is playing a shot, you shouldn't be playing the game.

What we have tried to do is take the legal speak of *The Rules of Golf* and convert it to language that anyone can understand. The basics of etiquette are also covered, and as a bonus we threw in a few pieces of advice that only sophisticated, experienced players know. Call it local knowledge.

234 How to determine when you've addressed the ball

Except in a hazard, a ball is considered addressed when you've taken your stance and grounded your club. Until that time, if the ball moves there is no penalty and it must be played from its new position. Once the ball is addressed, however, if it moves you incur a one-stroke penalty and the ball must be replaced before playing the next stroke. —RON KASPRISKE

235 How to determine a drop zone

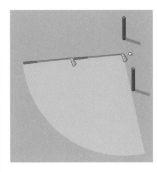

Any time you're about to drop, you need to understand that you can play your next shot from an area, not just from one precise spot. The area is determined by the type of drop you're about to take. For example, say your ball went into a lateral water hazard (which is marked by red stakes or lines). First, determine the point where your ball crossed the hazard. Then, using any club to measure the distance, drop and play your next shot within two club-lengths of that spot (as long as the ball is no closer to the hole than the point where it crossed the hazard). With most drops, you'll notice that this procedure creates a drop zone that is shaped like a pie wedge. —RON KASPRISKE

236 What you need to know about your putting line

In some instances, you're allowed to touch the line of your putt on a green. That line is defined as the path you believe your ball needs to travel in order to reach the hole. It includes some space on either side of that line but doesn't extend past the hole.

Here are the dos and don'ts:

• You can't touch the line with your hand to indicate the putt's path or to test the surface.

• You *can* touch the line to place or lift a ball marker.

• You *can* touch the line to remove loose impediments such as leaves and pebbles.

• You can't stand on the line or an extension of the line behind the ball while you putt.

• You can't touch the line to repair a spike mark.

• You *can* touch the line to shoo a bug. —RON KASPRISKE

237 How to determine when you've made a stroke

You have made a stroke when you make a forward motion toward the ball with the intent to hit it. A backswing is not considered the start of a stroke, nor is it considered a stroke if you intentionally stop your swing before hitting a ball, since your last intention was to *not* hit the ball. Note: If you are not on the tee and make a practice swing that accidentally hits the ball, it's not considered a stroke, but you are penalized one stroke for moving a ball in play, and the ball must be replaced. —RON KASPRISKE

238 How to mark your ball

There is no hard-and-fast rule. As long as you put the ball back on the spot where it was lifted, you can mark your ball with any object and in any manner you choose. But *The Rules of Golf* offers guidelines. The book suggests that the ball mark should be a coin or a similarly shaped object. We recommend that it not be shiny or distracting to other players. As for marking, the coin or object should be placed immediately behind the ball in reference to the hole.

—RON KASPRISKE

239 What to do when a ball moves on the putting green

If the ball moves after you have addressed it on a green—which means after you have taken your stance *and* grounded your putter—then you are penalized one stroke and the ball needs to be replaced. If you haven't addressed the ball and it moves (say, from a gust of wind), then play it from its new position. —RON KASPRISKE

240 How to drop a ball

Rule 20-2 says a player must stand straight, extend the arm at shoulder height, and let the ball drop. The act of flicking, tossing, or manipulating the drop in any way is a one-stroke penalty in stroke or match play. —RON KASPRISKE

241 How to play by "winter rules"

According to *The Rules of Golf,* there is no such thing as winter rules. A tournament committee or course manager, however, can enact "lift, clean, and place" rules for a round when conditions severely affect play. In those cases, the ball may be picked up, cleaned, and replaced in the spot where it came to rest without penalty.

— RON KASPRISKE

242 How to determine "the nearest point of relief"

In almost all cases, the nearest point of relief is determined by finding the spot that is no closer to the hole than where your ball came to rest, and that allows you to stand and swing without interference from the spot or object that prompted you to drop. The nearest point of relief is usually the starting point for an area that is triangular in shape, typically determined by one club-length, in which you may drop or place the ball.　— RON KASPRISKE

243 What to do when the ball falls off the tee

There is no penalty when this happens. Simply re-tee and play on.

—RON KASPRISKE

244 What to do if you think your ball is out of bounds

A ball is out of bounds when the entire ball is off the golf course, as defined by white stakes or lines. If any part of the ball is touching the boundary line, then the ball is considered in bounds.

Here are your options if you think the ball is out of bounds:

1. Before leaving the spot where your shot was played, declare that you are going to hit a provisional ball. Hit the shot, and then look for the original ball to determine if it is out of bounds. If it is, then the provisional ball becomes your ball in play and you add a penalty stroke to your score and also count the stroke taken with the provisional ball.

2. Take a one-stroke penalty and hit again from the spot where you just hit the shot out of bounds. In addition to the penalty stroke, all of the strokes you played also count.   —RON KASPRISKE

245 How to proceed when your ball hits a power line

You're 236 yards out on a par 5 and you hit your 3-wood flush. But as it tracks toward the green, it hits a power line and bounces into the rough. What do you do? Decision 33-8/13 says the course can enact a local rule requiring you to replay the shot without penalty. If the course doesn't have this local rule, play the ball as it lies.

—RON KASPRISKE

How to spot a hustler

About to make a bet with someone new? Here are some telltale signs he's a hustler:

> Before he introduces himself, he tells you about his sciatica.

> And when he does say his name, it's a state or city.

> You ask if he has ever seen the golf scene in *Goldfinger* and his reply is "Amateur hour."

> He peels off a $100 bill to pay for a hot dog.

> He claims the electronic ankle bracelet he's wearing is for his arthritis.

> You offer to help him search for his ball in the woods and he says, "I'm good. It really opens up in there."

> Every time you ask for his score on a hole, he says, "Why, what did you have?"

> His cell-phone ring tone is "The Entertainer," from the movie *The Sting*.

> The beverage-cart girl says, "You drinking the usual, Al?"

> You mention that you were watching *Meet the Press* on NBC yesterday and he blurts out, "Press? Did you say you want to press?"   —RON KASPRISKE

246 What to do when your ball is unplayable

Under Rule 28, as long as the ball is on the course and not in a water hazard, and you have identified it, you can declare it "unplayable." Then your options are:

1. Play your next shot from where the ball was last played (add a stroke penalty).

2. Keeping the spot of the unplayable lie directly between you and the hole, drop a ball as far back as you want (add a stroke penalty).

3. Drop a ball within two club-lengths of the unplayable lie, but no closer to the hole (add a stroke penalty).

Remember: you can use any club to determine the club-lengths. If you are taking an unplayable lie in a bunker and choose option two or three, you must take the drop in the bunker. If your ball is stuck in a tree, you can proceed under option three and drop within two club-lengths of the spot on the ground immediately below the ball, no closer to the hole, even if it's on the putting green.

—RON KASPRISKE

247 What to do if your ball stops on a cart path

Unless the path is designated as an integral part of the course (sometimes paths made of packed sand or wood chips are in play), it is considered an immovable obstruction and you are entitled to move your ball off the path without penalty. To do this correctly, determine the nearest spot from where the ball came to rest that is no closer to the hole and also provides you with enough room to stand and swing without interference from the path.

Keep in mind that the club you're using for the next shot will affect how much space you need. It also matters whether you are swinging left-handed or right-handed. But from this spot you are entitled to take a drop in an area that is within one club-length but no closer to the hole. —RON KASPRISKE

248　What to do when your ball is lost under leaves

On those fall days when leaves are dropping all over the course, the first thing you should do is check with the course to see if it's using a local rule that treats the accumulation of leaves as ground under repair (Decision 33-8/31). On designated holes, you might be entitled to relief without penalty if your ball stops in a leaf pile. Furthermore, if there is reasonable evidence that a ball entered a pile but is lost, a player can substitute another ball without penalty and drop it at the spot where the lost ball is believed to have crossed into the leaf pile. However, you must be certain the ball could not have been lost for any other reason. If you're not certain, treat it as a lost ball (Rule 27), take a one-stroke penalty, and replay the shot.

—RON KASPRISKE

249 What to do when your ball is in a water hazard

Unlike a lateral water hazard, a water hazard is marked with yellow stakes or lines. Here are your options for proceeding if you hit into one:

• Play the shot as it lies. But don't ground the club or it's a two-shot penalty.

• Replay the previous shot.

• Take a drop on the backward extension of the line from the hole to the entry point.

NOTE: The last two of these come with a one-stroke penalty.

—RON KASPRISKE

250 What to do when your ball is in ground under repair

Ground under repair (GUR) is typically marked with a white line or sign. If your ball, stance, or swing makes or would make contact with GUR, you are entitled to relief. Take a free drop within one club-length of the nearest point of relief, but not nearer the hole. Under definitions in *The Rules of Golf,* any material on a golf course piled for removal can be considered ground under repair by course or tournament officials, as was the case at the 2004 Masters, when Ernie Els hit his tee shot into a pile of branches next to the eleventh hole. But that doesn't mean any loose grass clippings left by a lawn mower should be treated as GUR. They have to be piled for removal.

—RON KASPRISKE

251 How to drop a ball on the opposite margin of a hazard

Perhaps the least understood option for taking a penalty drop after hitting a ball into a lateral water hazard (marked with red stakes or lines) is the drop on the "opposite margin," as stated in Rule 26-1c (ii). If your ball crosses into a lateral water hazard, you're allowed to find a point on the opposite side of the hazard that's the same distance from the hole as the point where your ball crossed the hazard. From there, you're allowed to take a drop within two club-lengths—but no closer to the hole. Add a penalty stroke and play on.

One caveat: If you draw an imaginary straight line from the point where your ball entered the hazard to that point on the opposite side of the hazard and that line first crosses land that is outside the hazard, then dropping on the opposite side is not an option.

—RON KASPRISKE

252 What to do when your ball is in a lateral water hazard

A lateral water hazard is marked with red stakes or lines, and you have several options on how to proceed should you hit your ball into one:

• Play the ball as it lies. But don't ground your club or it's a two-shot penalty.

• Replay the previous shot.

• Take a drop within two club-lengths of the spot where the ball crossed over the margin of the hazard, but no closer to the hole.

• Take a drop within two club-lengths, but no closer to the hole, from a point on the opposite side of the hazard, equidistant to the hole from where the ball last crossed the hazard margin.

• Take a drop behind the hazard, keeping the point where the ball last crossed the hazard on an imaginary line with the hole. You can drop anywhere on an extension of that line, as long as it is no closer to the hole.

NOTE: All of these, except the first, come with a one-stroke penalty.

—RON KASPRISKE

253 How to play a shot from jail

You are allowed to move loose impediments such as pine straw, stones, dead leaves on the ground, etc., provided your ball does not move in the process. You cannot remove or break anything fixed or growing, such as branches, leaves still attached to trees, grass blades, etc., unless the item comes loose while taking your stance. When making a practice swing, do not break any branches. However, it is permissible for damage to occur to a growing or fixed object while making the swing. —RON KASPRISKE

254 What to do when your ball in play is taken

That someone or something that took your ball is referred to as an "outside agency." It can be a ball-hawking golfer, a squirrel, a dog—anything that moves your ball and is not part of your match. If you are reasonably sure someone has taken your ball, you are entitled to take a drop as close as possible to the spot where your ball was lost but no closer to the hole. There is no penalty, but you have to be positive the ball couldn't have been lost in another manner. If it was lost, you have to replay the previous shot with a one-stroke penalty.

—RON KASPRISKE

255 What to do when your ball is damaged or scuffed

You need to alert your opponent or playing partner of your intent to remove and replace the ball in play. The other person has an opportunity to inspect the ball and can dispute the claim if he feels the ball is still suitable for play. A scuffed ball is not considered damaged enough to be removed. The ball must be cracked, cut, or warped. — RON KASPRISKE

256 What to do when you break or lose a club

If you lose a club, it cannot be replaced until the round is complete unless you started with fewer than fourteen clubs, the maximum number permitted.

If you break a club, it can be replaced unless the damage occurred outside the normal course of play. This also means it can be replaced if you leaned on it and it accidentally broke, or was damaged, say, when you tried to remove it from the golf bag. But the club has to be replaced without unduly delaying play.

If the damage occurred because you threw the club, slammed it, or did anything unintentionally in an act that isn't considered to be part of the normal course of play, the club cannot be replaced. — RON KASPRISKE

257 What to do when a club is bent or altered

A club that is purposely bent or altered so that its playing characteristics have changed must be taken out of play. If you started with fourteen clubs—the maximum allowed—it cannot be replaced until the round is complete. —RON KASPRISKE

258 How to let people play through

If there is no group directly in front of you, then strongly consider letting a group play through when they are waiting on you. The best place to do this is on a par 3. Hit your tee shots, mark your balls, and then wave the next group up. It's a good idea to stand off to the side—not just for protection but also because you don't want to distract the other golfers. While the group approaches the green, you can go ahead and putt out or wait until they are clear. Letting another group play through is not a matter of pride. If you insist on playing slowly, don't make others suffer. —RON KASPRISKE

259 What to do when your shot hits someone

Fact is, when you're in the wrong, you're in the wrong. Get to the scene of the accident as fast as you can. Run. Check if the guy is OK, and, if necessary, call an ambulance. Apologize deeply, widely, and often, until you're told to shut up. Attempt to explain the situation. Offer lunch and drinks for the entire group. Apologize again.

260 What to do when you think your opponent cheated

If you have evidence, confront the cheater with it. Friendly match? No such thing if cheaters are involved. Cheating is the woodworm in the foundation that civilization is built on, and it must be squashed.

261 What to do when you're losing big in a golf bet

A bet is a bet. Pay up. And don't ever get into a jam like this again; your days of trying to be a high roller are over. What's that you say? You really can't afford to pay? You're willing to lose all your credibility by trying to worm out of the debt? OK, fine. Perhaps dignity in this situation might be overrated. So come clean: tell the guy things got out of hand and you've gotten in way over your head. Apologize, plead, and beg. Try to negotiate down the debt or figure out a more manageable payment plan. And say, "I don't want to fall out over this. How about I take you for a first-rate meal at that steak house down the road once a month for the next year?" If the guy won't budge, however, you have no choice but to take out that loan. Game—and friendship—over. Lesson learned.

262 How to behave when your game goes to pieces

Your golf swing, in the words of Prince Charles describing his ill-fated marriage to Diana Spencer, has "irretrievably broken down." So what? Get over yourself. There's absolutely no reason your miserable golf should make anyone else miserable. It's your job to make sure your group has a good time. Humor will save the day. A carefully prepared arsenal of self-deprecating remarks will deflect the shame, embarrassment, and sheer misery of chronic bad play:

> "Sorry guys, I'm about as useless as an ashtray on a motorcycle."

> "I'm about as much use as a one-legged man in an ass-kicking contest."

Manage your poor play as the best you can. Lower your expectations and play smart. Ask for swing tips, say nice things about the others' play, and pick up when you're out of the hole. Never get angry, and keep those one-liners coming. This is a test. Pass with dignity.

263 How to behave after you just hit a pitiful tee shot

Hitting a foozle off the first tee is one of the greatest fears known to humankind. But the fact is, it has happened to everyone who has ever played the game. Over the years, we've seen many of the best golfers in the world hit terrible, hugely embarrassing duffs in front of thousands of people (and sometimes TV cameras too). OK, you knew all that already but still hit a horrendous dribbler. At this point, you could take a bow, or crack a joke to the assembled gathering, or pretend there's something wrong with your driver (closely examine the clubhead). But it's better simply to accept what happened and then do what you should always do in golf, regardless of the situation: focus on the next shot. Don't take a mulligan, even if offered, or pick the ball up. Don't panic. Don't rush. Relax—no one cares about your lousy shot. Accept it, stand tall, and move forward the best way you can.

264 How to deal with a racist/ bigot/jerk stranger

You can't play with this guy. If you choose to tell him why, so much the better. But maybe actions can speak louder than words. Pick up your bag and tell the starter you'd like to play with some different people—preferably ones who don't still live in a cave.

If it takes a few holes for the lunkhead to reveal himself, then you should play on until the turn and excuse yourself after nine holes, saying you had an appointment or a family emergency. No need to be rude, but you don't have to be warm and fuzzy either.

265 How to get past a dreadfully slow foursome of big men

Ask the meatheads in a loud, confident voice if you can play through. Explain that you're in a rush and you'll be out of their way in no time. For the next few seconds, hold your ground and observe them very closely. If they start to bristle, or crack their knuckles, or remove concealed weapons from about their personages, quickly say, "Tell you what, if you let us through the drinks are on us in the clubhouse when you're done. I swear we'll be out of your way in five minutes." If they still don't budge, retreat, give yourself net par for that hole, and head straight for the next tee box. You could also complain to the ranger, but beware: those Cro-Magnon types can't stand a tattletale.

266 What to do when you really gotta go and there's no bathroom in sight

You're pretty sure you can't make the rest of the back nine without causing some sort of internal injury. So you gotta go—when nature calls, nature must be answered. First, scan the landscape. Is there really nowhere with a modicum of privacy to take care of business? It's not a big deal, if you're discreet about it. Second, take a look at the course map and see if any upcoming holes pass close to the clubhouse. If all else fails, tell the group you left your wallet back at the halfway house and need to go get it and you'll catch up with them later. Whatever you do, don't suffer in silence. We don't want any accidents out there.

267 How to play golf with a caddie

As a former caddie at St. Andrews, I can tell you that people who have never taken a caddie are sometimes made uncomfortable by the relationship. They shouldn't be. A looper's top priority is to make your round more enjoyable, and getting on a caddie's good side is easy. Insist that the caddie call you by your first name. Tell him to stow the driver and putter covers in the bag. Offer to buy snacks at the turn. Discuss each shot with him, no matter how briefly and regardless of your ability. These little exchanges put you in the routine of positively envisioning your shot. Tremendous psychological benefit can be tapped from the mere gestures shared with a caddie. And when the round is done, tip with the bills folded or rolled and exchanged discreetly. That's the classy way. —MAX ADLER

268 What to do when the big boss violates your club's rules

Some people think club rules are quaint holdovers from the nineteenth century and are not really meant to be observed. Others think they're open to interpretation. Is a BlackBerry a cell phone, for instance? Mr. Big, however, is clearly breaking a rule when he tries to use his cell phone at your country club. They've been banned from use on the premises. This isn't your rule—it's a club rule. You should have called Mr. Big on it in the locker room—it's always best to "bend the twig while it's green," as the saying goes. Now you have no choice but to march right up to him on the fairway and tell him: "Boss, they're really strict about cell phones around here. They're forbidden. I know it's crazy, but if you get caught, I might be looking to join another club. So could you help me out and not use the cell today?" Get close physically. Close talking conveys a sense of urgency. If he persists, you'll just have to suck it up for the rest of the day if you don't want to get fired. Throw yourself on the mercy of the club president. Chances are you'll only get a letter of reprimand.

How to play golf forever

People often ask me why I enjoy playing golf so much. I tell them it's because I have these rules I follow—rules I try never to break, except when money is involved.

Here are the rules to follow if you want to play better and live longer:

1. Never play golf with a guy who keeps a tee behind his ear (it's the same reason I don't smoke with a guy who carries a cigarette behind his ear).

2. Never play golf with a guy who carries a towel to the green (adds an hour to the round).

3. Never play golf with a guy whose headcovers resemble Disney characters.

4. Never play couples golf.

5. Never play golf with a guy who wears more than one golf wrist bracelet (he has a cell phone you haven't seen—yet—and will make thirty-seven calls before you reach the ninth green).

6. Never play golf with a guy who keeps personal stats.

7. Never play golf with a guy who has one of those bags with separate compartments for all his irons.

8. Never play golf with a guy whose nickname is stitched into his bag. —DAN JENKINS

269 How to get through a round without pissing anyone off

There's basic etiquette—stuff like not walking in someone's putting line and being quiet when someone is hitting—and then there's advanced etiquette. Once you have the basic stuff down, you're ready for these rules to advance etiquette.

• Don't give golf lessons. Unless you are David Leadbetter, never give an impromptu lesson during a round. First of all, you're not that good. Second, you're not that good.

• Stay back. When a group is on the tee, don't pull up to that tee box until that group is clear.

• Be ready to hit. Go to your ball instead of waiting in the cart or next to the person whose turn it is to hit.

• Tend the flag. Always ask members of the group if they need the flag tended when they have a long putt.

• Keep an extra ball in your pocket. If you lose one, it slows play too much if you have to go back to your bag for another.

• No plumb bobbing. A pointless putting-alignment procedure. If you don't know what it is, forget we ever mentioned it.

• Putt out. Don't mark if your first putt stops near the hole.

• Be sensitive. If you're keeping the scorecard and someone has a bad hole, wait a bit before asking his or her score.

• One or two practice swings only.

• Stop searching. The USGA gives you five minutes to find a lost ball. In most cases, if you don't find it in two minutes move on.

• Get to the punch line. Jokes are good only if there's a wait on the fairway.

• Let the single through. We've all been that guy trying to get in a quick nine alone. He won't slow you down.

• Leave our clubs alone. Unless you see a tarantula climb onto our 3-wood, keep your paws off our clubs without permission.

• Stop talking. No need to comment on every shot—especially when we hit a bad one.

• Pay up. You lost the bet. We don't care why. Just have money handy.

— RON KASPRISKE

270 How to rake a bunker

We asked PGA Tour caddies for the correct way to rake a bunker after playing a shot. Here are their tips:

1. Use your foot to level out club marks and footprints.

2. Turn the rake upside down and push the sand forward.

3. Turn the rake over and skim the top of the sand as you pull toward you. Keep the rake handle low.

4. Push the rake toward the hole.

271   How to repair a pitch mark

If you're new to golf, you might not know that it's considered good etiquette to repair the small crater your ball makes when it lands on the green. Here's a three-step method:

1. Insert the divot tool or tee around the base of the pitch mark, but not so deep that it severs grass roots.

2. Make a gentle twisting motion around the edges of the crater so the grass gets pushed back into the middle and fills the divot.

3. Tap down on the mark.   —RON KASPRISKE

272   What score you should record when you make a ten on a hole

You just made a ten on a hole, and you vaguely remember that you can't post a ten when you record your round in the handicap computer. So what score do you post? There is something in golf called Equitable Stroke Control, or ESC. Under the USGA's ESC system, players with course handicaps of nine or less can post no higher than a double bogey on any hole. Handicappers in the 10–19 range can post a maximum of seven on any hole, 20–29 can take an eight, and 30–39 can take a nine.   —RON KASPRISKE

Helpful Skills

The intricacies of the game extend far beyond the white out-of-bounds stakes, and it can take decades to acquire enough wisdom to truly feel comfortable with any situation. This chapter is an attempt to help you handle several of the most common dilemmas and a few of the most bizarre ones too.

The intent is to give you a broad scope of knowledge—everything from repairing a ball mark to playing golf with the boss to tipping a caddie. Perhaps the biggest factor in enjoying the game is avoiding embarrassment.

273 How to play when you're beating the boss and he's getting mad

Bury the guy. Show no mercy. Put him away. Nobody likes a loser. But make sure you win with grace. No fist pumping. Thank him for the game and tell him you got lucky. When you get back to the office, assuming you still have a job, no public bragging. Golf is war. Never forget that.

274 How to pick the right golf instructor

Finding the best teacher can make or break your game. Good instructors are part scientist and part artist, according to sport psychologist Dick Coop. "Make sure your teacher knows enough about the golf swing so he's not experimenting on you," says Coop. "But just as important as knowing what to say is knowing when to say it." The best sessions are cooperative or interactive, a give-and-take in which the teacher is listening and adapting to your game, not just selling his or her pet method. "Good teachers don't teach the golf swing, they teach the golf swing to a specific person," says Coop.   — PETER MORRICE

275 How to perform a preshot routine like a pro

EDITOR'S NOTE: *The purpose of a preshot routine, pros will tell you, is to develop consistency and also to ensure that you are properly prepared to play a shot. While routines vary slightly from one pro to the next, the majority do something similar to what Colin Montgomerie says he does. Follow his steps:*

1. I start from a point about four paces behind the ball. From there, I pick the area of the fairway I want to hit. I picture the height, trajectory, and flight of the ball.

2. I walk slowly forward to the ball, still focusing on where I want the ball to go.

3. I make only one practice swing; I don't want to lose the picture of the shot in my mind. Then I go. I don't spend too long over the ball. Too much time at address leads to negative thoughts. Be positive! —COLIN MONTGOMERIE

276 How to know the best time to tee off

What is the ideal time to play? All things being equal, Ben Hogan knew that a 10 a.m. tee time meant greens that were typically devoid of footprints and spike marks. The dew had evaporated. Plus, you could work the ball better when the ball and clubs were dry. There are two more reasons for wanting the 10 a.m. tee time: it's late enough for the player to sleep in but not so early that he has to spend hours wondering what the day and his round will bring.

—JOHNNY MILLER

277 How to handle slow play

The great Canadian ball-striker Moe Norman played so fast that tournament officials sometimes asked him to slow down. In response, Norman devised various dilatory techniques: following a zigzag route to his ball, pretending to sleep while waiting for others to play, reading a book. At the 1956 Masters, he teed off before the starter had finished announcing his name.

So how does a fast player cope with slow play? A couple of years ago, in a two-man tournament at my club, my partner and I played a match in which one of our opponents was hopelessly slow. Rather than allowing his pace to get to me, I set myself the challenge of playing even slower than he did—a highly satisfying tactic, and one that kept my blood pressure well under par.

In another tournament, in which my own partner was the dawdler, I remained calm by taking delight in how thoroughly he was annoying our opponents. "Can't you do something?" one of them hissed at me at one point. I said I would try. A little later, as my partner was endlessly fussing over his club selection for a perfectly straightforward shot, I urged him, in a voice too low for our opponents to overhear, "Take your time."

—DAVID OWEN

278 How to spot a good caddie

Here are five things to look for in a caddie:

1. Knowledge of the course. Good reads, helpful targets on blind shots, accurate yardages.

2. Equipment service. Bag clean and organized, grips dry during inclement weather. The caddie should handle the umbrella.

3. Time management. He should get to the ball before you do.

4. A high level of interest in your game. Does he know how you stand in the match?

5. Knowledge of rules and etiquette. — MAX ADLER

279 How to get the most out of a caddie

As longtime PGA Tour caddie for Tom Kite, I don't mean to toot my own horn, but a good caddie can make all the difference in the world. Obviously, you shouldn't expect the same from a beginning youngster that you might from a tour caddie, but within reason they should have a number of things in common.

A caddie should be prompt, dependable, clean, and neat. None of that takes any special training. A caddie should keep your clubs clean and be aware of proper yardages. A good local caddie will also be able to read greens, as well as alert you to any unique local conditions, such as swirling winds, etc. Caddies should also know the rules, so that you are not inadvertently penalized by one of his mistakes, such as leaving the bag where it can be hit with your ball or touching the putting surface when indicating the line.

It's not fair to expect a caddie to be able to "club" you the first time out. Nobody is that good. Nor is it fair to be abusive to a caddie in any way, no matter how bad your round. In that light, I recall a sign I saw at a club that summed it all up well: "Treat your caddie as you would your son."
— MIKE CARRICK

280   What to do when your child is ready to play

When you feel that your child knows the rules, etiquette, and golf swing well enough to attempt a round on a golf course, follow these steps to make the day more enjoyable for the child and you:

• On a regulation course, have the child tee off from the 150-yard marker.

• Based on the child's ability, assign a customized par for each hole and a special scorecard to match.

• Visit the course at off-peak hours to avoid slowing down experienced players, and have the child pick up his or her ball if the score gets into double digits.

• Tee the ball in the fairway, and use clubs that have a lot of loft until the child gains confidence.

• Let the child try easier shots over water. Even if the ball doesn't carry the hazard, it's fun to watch it splash.

— RENEE POWELL

281 How to find a lost ball

The most common mistake golfers make when they've hit a ball into the boonies is throwing a fit instead of watching the ball. Follow the ball's flight and mark not only where it went into the junk but also how high up. Don't rely on memory. Mark the spot with an object that stands out, such as a bright bush, a tall tree, or a rock. Don't forget to listen for the sound of the ball hitting a tree. The more solid the sound, the farther the ball might have ricocheted.

When you begin to search, make sure you have a club with you to root the ball out of a place you can't reach and also for protection— seriously. No matter where you play, there's usually a snake indigenous to the area, and you might need the club to scare it off.

As you search for the ball, establish a pattern and stick with it. Just wandering around reduces your chances of finding the ball. Also, be aware that there is a five-minute limit on how long you can search. Oh, and if you're holding up other groups, let them play through.

—ANGELO ARGEA

282 How to play better as you get older

Amateur golfers often improve with age, because increased leisure time in their senior years allows them to play more frequently. But two other things can contribute to lower scores for seniors:

1. Sticking to a pattern of play. For instance, if you are a natural hooker or fader, go with the game you have and allow the shot to curve.

2. Using equipment that compensates for the slowing up of muscles and reflexes. Lighter woods and irons are recommended.

—JIMMY DEMARET

helpful skills

283 How to pick the best golf camp for Junior

If your child exhibits an avid interest in the game, you might want to consider sending him or her to a summer camp. When selecting a camp, look beyond price. Instead, consider camps that offer training in specific areas:

• Find a camp that teaches kids to use practice time wisely and economically. There should be drills that can be continued once they go home.

• Short-game instruction must be a priority. Competence in putting, chipping, and pitching determines how well kids can compete and how often they win.

• The camp should be appropriate for your child's skill level as well as for his or her personality.　　　　　— JIM FLICK

284 How to play golf with the boss

If you get an invite to play a round with your boss, here are some steps that will make the day less stressful and more enjoyable, and could possibly further your career:

1. Make the most of the opportunity. The boss will be watching to see how you perform under pressure as well as how you handle adversity. Don't throw clubs or swear. And follow etiquette rules, including repairing ball marks and replacing divots.

2. Make preparations for the round without bothering the boss with unnecessary questions, such as how to get to the course. Wear something tasteful and within the dress code of the golf course.

3. Be prepared for intelligent conversation about world events, golf, etc., but don't talk business. Take your conversation cues from the boss. And don't drink too much.

4. Let the boss decide which type of game you will play. Play by the rules unless a mulligan is offered. And play to win. Don't try to throw the round. Win or lose with grace.

5. Write a handwritten note thanking the boss for the round. And don't talk about the round at the office. If others ask, just say you had a good time and offer little detail. If the boss talks about it, pay attention.

285 What to pack for a golf trip to Scotland

Scottish golf is probably unlike any you have ever played. And I'm not just talking about navigating the links-style courses or deciphering the instructions offered by a caddie with a thick accent. You will need to deal with extreme weather conditions that change quickly.

Invest in waterproof—not water-resistant—rain jackets and pants (Nike Golf, Adidas Golf, FootJoy's DryJoys, and Zero Restriction all make good ones). They can handle rougher weather conditions. If you're wide and short, pick rain trousers that can be shortened. Wear your golf shoes when you try on rain trousers so they can be hemmed to the appropriate length. And keep in mind that you'll be walking at St. Andrews, and many other Scottish links, so go for trousers that are light and have belt loops so they won't drop when they get waterlogged. Another option is to wait until you get to Scotland so you can purchase a rain suit from Galvin Green, a great line that's not sold on this side of the pond. Just don't forget that things tend to be more expensive there, because pounds are worth more than dollars. Oh, and bring two pairs of golf shoes and a rain hat. — MARTY HACKEL

286 How to get on a very exclusive private course

EDITOR'S NOTE: *Steve Frank is not a member of many of the top courses in the country, but he has played most of them thanks to his skill in getting invitations that others don't. Here are some of his tips if you want to get past the gates and tee it up:*

• Become acquainted with or find a member who'll host you.

• Inquire whether the course is used for a charity event that is open to the public.

• Find out if the course is used as a local qualifying site for the USGA or a regional championship, and if your handicap is low enough, enter.

• Ask the director of golf if a nonmember can play the course during the off-season.

• Have the pro at your club call the pro at the other club. You might be able to play at an off-peak time.

• Does the club have a tie-in with a hotel, which accords limited playing privileges?

- Take lessons from the club's professional, and after getting acquainted ask for a playing lesson.
- If you're retired or have the spare time, try getting a part-time job at the club, which might include Monday playing privileges.
- Volunteer at a major tournament. Volunteers are sometimes allowed to play the course after the event.
- Always be courteous. — STEVE FRANK

287 How to dress like a golfer

Dressing well has much to do with attitude. Outgoing people with strong personalities can wear bolder colors and trendier styles better (see Ian Poulter). Proportion is key, so if you are tall and thin select stripes that are thin. Bigger people should keep the colors in the same tone, so all black works well on Phil Mickelson. And remember to keep the belt color the same as your shirt or slacks, like Adam Scott does. Nothing looks worse than a black belt with khakis and a white shirt (if you're slim you might get away with it). Wear your trousers around your waist and avoid letting them get too low—this will de-emphasize your waist.

— MARTY HACKEL

288 How to store your golf glove while playing

When it's time during a round to take your golf glove off—typically when you putt—either tuck it into your back pocket so the fingers are exposed or fold it in half and put it into your front pocket. You don't want to bunch the glove up or put it into your pocket with the fingers down, since they're dirty and will soil your pants or shorts. —MARTY HACKEL

289 How to cope with a slump

You cannot play golf for any length of time without having a head-on encounter with a slump. If you go a half-dozen rounds without scoring within five strokes of your handicap, you're in a slump. Pros will tell you there are several methods of coping with a slump:

- Ignore it.
- Quit playing for a while.
- Analyze it.
- Practice more.
- Practice less, or not at all.
- Work on only the short game.
- See a teaching pro.

My favorite advice, though, comes from Patty Berg: "Start building your game all over. Practice with short irons first until you are hitting them right. Then work up to longer clubs." —BETTY HICKS

290 How to make your practice time smarter

The best players give full focus to every practice shot. None of their practice time is just mindless ball beating.

• Treat every practice shot as if it were a shot during a real round. For example, pick a specific target and distance. Most amateurs look for the ball to go straight, but they don't pick a target or pay attention to whether the shot goes the correct distance.

• Don't become obsessed with hitting the ball perfectly. You ever notice how you can hit a bad drive on one hole and make par and kill your drive on another and make bogey? It's hard for people to comprehend.

• Not all short shots are equally important. If you asked me how to hit a fifty-yard bunker shot, I would say, "Why do you care?" You might face that shot once a year. Instead of practicing it, learn to avoid it. Instead, focus on shots from 70 to 120 yards and inside of 15 yards.

• Spend most of your time pitching fifteen yards or less. Go on a mission to become a great pitcher of the ball.

• Don't treat putting practice like a job. The best way to practice putting is to play competitive games on the green.

—BOB ROTELLA AND HANK HANEY

291 How to watch Tiger play a round

Getting up close to the world's greatest golfer is a lot like getting close to Oscar nominees on the red carpet. A little planning and good timing, and you'll catch more than a glimpse. Here are a few suggestions:

• If it's a practice round, Tiger almost always plays at first light, so get to the course before sunrise.

• If it's a regular round, use the three-holes-ahead method and you should get to see him five or six times. After you watch him play through, jump ahead three holes to another viewing spot. Note: Standing behind him when he tees off with a driver is something every golf fan should do at least once.

• Late in the day, go to the driving range. There's a decent chance he'll be one of the guys out there practicing—especially at the majors.

— RON KASPRISKE

292 How to watch a tour event

• Get a course map (they can usually be found at the tournament entrance) and try to locate the hole farthest from the clubhouse. Most people will be too lazy to walk all the way out there, so you will have great access to the players and the action at this spot.

• Find a spot where three or more holes are in view. Watch two groups tee off at the same time.

• Follow a good group of golfers around at the same time that Tiger is on the opposite nine. You might be alone.   —RON KASPRISKE

How not to be an ugly American

Despite what you might have heard, people throughout most of the civilized world love vacationing Americans. The traveling Yank provides insight into transatlantic clothing trends, opportunities for discussions about world affairs, and, of course, really big tips. To do your bit for international relations, here are some simple rules of etiquette:

1. Speed: In America, golf is slow and food is fast. In Europe, it's the opposite. Get used to it.

2. Volume: Americans have a reputation for being loud. Try to dispel this by being the quiet American.

3. Dress: Take your hat off indoors. Anywhere.

4. Whining: If you don't like it, stay home.

5. Caddies: Treat them with the greatest respect. Be polite, chatty, and generous with your tip.

6. Swearing: If you are concerned about causing offense, substitute the word with something harmless. Scottish town names are good: Ecclefechan, Auchtermuchty, or Pool of Muckhart.

7. Relieving oneself: The problem with British links is the lack of trees. Keep your equipment out of view of passing motorists, dog walkers, and lady golfers.   —JOHN BARTON

helpful skills

189

293 How to get Tiger's autograph

The best time to obtain an autograph from Tiger Woods is after practice rounds. After those rounds, stand near the gallery ropes that run from the eighteenth green to the practice range and the clubhouse. He will often pause after playing and practicing, usually signing as he walks. Woods loves kids and tries to accommodate as many as he can. He doesn't like to be pushed or have objects shoved in his face, so get close to the ropes and use proper etiquette. He also hates it when young kids serve as runners to collect autographs for adults to sell, and he's very good at spotting them. It doesn't hurt to stand out. Consider wearing colorful clothing or a Tiger costume to get his attention. He gets a kick out of seeing people dress up and will often make a point of signing for them.

Sometimes Tiger will sign autographs after he has finished playing tournament rounds. During those rounds, the three things to keep in mind are persistence, patience, and position. Don't scream his name; let him make eye contact with you and be ready to walk as he signs. Eventually, your efforts will be rewarded.   —MARK SOLTAU

294 How to get your favorite golfer's autograph

The sad truth is that it's a lot harder to get autographs today than it was in past eras. Many golfers are reluctant to sign because the fans who approach them aren't polite and their signatures often end up on eBay. However, it's far from impossible. Here are some tips:

• Know when and where to ask: after practice rounds is best.

• Know your pro: to get the attention of someone like Ernie Els, say something specific about his career, college, or interests.

• Let your kid do the talking: tour players will often sign only for children.

• Bring a permanent marker and something easy to sign.

• Ask a player to make it out to your name. The pro will be more likely to sign, because he or she will be less likely to think you're going to sell the autograph online.

• If all else fails, send a request letter to the PGA Tour or LPGA Tour. They'll almost always forward the request.　　—RON KASPRISKE

295　How to improve your chances of getting a tee time

When you call for a tee time, have a time in mind. You wouldn't believe how many people want me to read off every available tee time for the day. We also get people asking what the pace of play is. Hello? It could change three times in one day. How should I know? The best days to play are Mondays, Tuesdays, and whatever day at your course is Ladies' Day, because that usually scares off players who think women are slow. They're not.

How do you get a good tee time on a weekend? Call me or

check online the minute times become available. If you're thinking of calling last-minute, you're better off showing up the morning you want to play and asking to be squeezed in—even a foursome. Most courses want the revenue, so they'll do their best to get you on.

And if I get you a tee time, don't stiff me by not showing up. I know who you are and I won't forget.

— ANONYMOUS PRO

296 What to do if you didn't get a tee time but still want to play

If you didn't secure a tee time with the pro in the shop and you're hoping to play an unannounced round, then the starter is the link between you and the first tee.

Some tips to improve your chances of getting on the course:

• Be prepared, and have the players in your group arrive early and be ready to play when they are called.

• Don't attempt to get preferential treatment.

• Don't attempt to charm the starter. He or she has heard it all before.

• Don't repeatedly ask, "Where am I on the waiting list?" Probably the same place you were when you inquired about the starting time five minutes earlier.

• Don't ask, "How long will it take me to get out?"

• Don't try to grease the starter to improve your odds. Bribes can backfire.

• Don't ask whether it's going to rain. The starter is not a meteorologist, and he or she might think you will flake out and leave if the weather turns bad. You're in this for the long haul.

— JOHN STREGE

297 How to become a tour caddie

If you're interested in carrying a bag on the PGA Tour, veteran caddies Scott Gneiser, Mike Carrick, and Jim MacKay offer their advice:

"Go to the Nationwide Tour and try to hook up with a young pro," says MacKay. Adds Gneiser, "It used to be that you could just hang out at PGA Tour stops and pick up a bag if the player's usual caddie wasn't there. And who knows? You might end up staying out there once you got some experience—but not anymore. Today, everyone on tour brings out their friends and family to caddie for them." Adds Carrick, "You also need experience. You need to know a lot of the little stuff before you even get to the pro level. It's not like the old days where you can learn as you go. You need to caddie for a lot of people with a lot of different personalities, learn how to read a yardage book, and know the number your player wants before he even asks for it."

— RON KASPRISKE

298 How to get invited back to a country club

You finally got to play that really nice private course. Want to play it again someday? Follow these steps and you will greatly improve your chances:

1. Wear your dressiest golf outfit. Shorts are OK, but make sure they're Bermuda length and aren't wrinkled. And no cargo shorts or cargo pants!

2. Ask about the club's tipping policy before you go and have cash ready. Allow the member to pay for everything, but offer to pay your caddie fee and also take care of your gratuities.

3. Never change your golf shoes in the parking lot. Ask the locker-room attendant, or your host, for a locker.

4. Always take your hat off indoors. If your hair is a mess, grab one of those combs in the blue water and fix it or take a shower.

5. Take care of the course as if it were your front lawn.

6. Don't throw clubs, play slow, or get into an argument with anyone.

7. If you're staying for dinner, bring a change of clothes, including a sport coat or a blazer or a cocktail dress. —RON KASPRISKE

299 How to pack for a long golf trip

Don't leave home without these key items.

• Painkillers: Advil, Aleve, Tylenol, scotch. Be advised, however, that only time can heal the pain of missing that two-footer.

• Sunblock: Alcohol-based sprays are better than lotions. Ever have a tube explode in your luggage?

• Camera: Nothing fancy, just good enough to document key moments like Joe passing out in the parking lot at Denny's.

• Lots of socks and underwear: Change frequently, please.

• Cigars: Make sure they're fresh, don't crush them in a suitcase, and smoke upwind.

• Laptop: Not for work. It's great to have one for looking up things like weather reports, directions, and, in rare cases, the nearest hospital.

• Bottle opener and corkscrew: You can't carry them on a plane anymore, so pack them.

• Breakfast/energy bars: Quick snacks between meals come in handy when you're playing thirty-six a day.

• DVDs: *Caddyshack* or the '86 Masters preferred.

- Cell-phone charger.

- Bug spray: We recommend anything with DEET.

- Band-Aids or athletic tape: Golf marathons = blisters.

- Deck of cards: Real golfers play gin rummy. Texas Hold'em has become more overexposed than Paris Hilton.

- Two extra golf gloves: By Day Three, especially if it rains, the first one will look as if you've been doing oil changes with it.

- Earplugs or an iPod or noise-canceling headphones: Ever hear a middle-aged man snore after two bottles of cabernet, or a teething child on a long flight?

- A second pair of golf shoes: Sneaker types are best. They're comfy, and by the end of the week no one cares what you look like.

- A lot of one-dollar and five-dollar bills: And not for the strip club. These are for the starter, the maid, the club cleaner. Don't be stingy.

- Tiger Balm: Some part of your anatomy (no need to share) is going to be killing you after a few days. This is our favorite topical analgesic.

- *Decisions on the Rules of Golf:* Trust us.　　—RON KASPRISKE

300　How to keep the locker-room attendant happy

Most people don't understand what a locker-room attendant does. It's more than shining shoes. I keep the bathrooms clean, replace spikes, make sure there are fresh towels and Advil handy and that the TV is always on the right channel. I'll even get you a drink while you clean up. In return, all I expect is to be treated politely and be thanked with more than a buck or two. A five-dollar tip is the minimum, ten dollars is fair, and twenty dollars if I went out of my way to make your day enjoyable. A few pet peeves:

• Don't throw your towels in the garbage bin or your garbage in the towel bin.

• If you want your street shoes shined, leave them in front of your locker.

• Give me a little time to clean up your golf shoes after the round. Don't stand there and wait.

• If you want something, just ask. Don't expect me to be a mind reader. —ANONYMOUS LOCKER-ROOM ATTENDANT

301 How to mow your lawn like a golf course

Brad Owen, the super-intendent at Augusta National, offers these tips for taking care of your lawn:

• It's best to let your yard dry out before watering it. Excessive watering encourages disease and weeds.

• You'll save water and improve your results if you water trouble spots by hand rather than always soaking the entire lawn. Watch the weather forecast and turn off your sprinkler system when rain is on the way.

• Don't cut grass by more than 30 percent in one mowing. Removing too much of the blade at once causes stress and promotes disease.

• Sharpen the blades of your mower a few times a year. Sharp blades cut grass instead of tearing it, and that's better for the grass.

• Have your soil tested, and ask local environmentalists for advice specific to your soil type and your region. —DAVID OWEN

302 What to remember before taking a golf bet

Laying money in golf is a science. I claim you haven't been educated until you know the betting angles. There are many helpful tips, but these three rules are the ones you have to remember:

1. Never gamble with a stranger.

2. If someone offers to take fewer shots and up the wager, back away fast.

3. Never risk more than you can afford. —SAM SNEAD

303 What to buy a golfer for his or her birthday

To most people who play the game, two dozen high-end golf balls are as exciting a gift as any watch, MP3 player, or cashmere sweater. Free golf balls—especially the kind tour players use—are like free money.

You can always go the extra step and get the birthday boy or girl some personalized golf balls. Most manufacturers offer this service for an extra six to ten dollars per dozen. It takes a few weeks for delivery. —STINA STERNBERG

304 How to play golf wearing glasses

Whether you wear shades to protect your eyes from the sun or glasses to help you see distant objects, your biggest problem is going to be keeping your lenses clear.

When playing in hot, muggy weather, I carry an extra towel strictly for cleaning my glasses. This helps solve the problem of fogging lenses. Before each shot, I take off my glasses, wipe my forehead and eyebrows well, check the glasses to make sure they're not fogged up, and then put them on and hit the shot.

When it's raining, I keep a dry towel inside the staves of my umbrella. Before every shot, I check my glasses while under the umbrella and wipe off any rain.

— MASON RUDOLPH

305 How to look cool when you make your first hole in one

Since 1971, when the PGA Tour began keeping track of holes in one in official events, no one has made more than Hal Sutton (ten). It's not enough to raise your arms when the ball goes in, says Sutton. His advice:

1. Let it out. This is the one time in golf that it's OK to jump around and shout.

2. You've got to finish the round to make it official, but take the ball out of play and save it.

3. You're buying a drink for everyone at the bar.

4. After the round, call every golfer you know. It's OK to gloat in this instance. — HAL SUTTON

306 How to take a good golf-course photograph

If you're playing Pebble Beach, Bandon Dunes, or St. Andrews and you want to take a few memorable photographs for your den or photo album, remember these pro tips from Stephen Szurlej, senior staff photographer at *Golf Digest:*

1. Sunshine is essential. If the sky is not blue and the sun is not bright enough to create distinct shadows, put your camera away and pull out the golf clubs.

2. Shoot only when the sun is low in the sky. Just after sunrise and an hour before sunset are ideal. The sun will be "warmest" in color quality at those times, and shadows from trees and undulating topography will be most pronounced. If you are playing during the middle of the day, consider taking pictures before or after the round, when the sun will be lower.

3. Bring your own elevation, especially if the course is flat. A twelve-to fourteen-foot stepladder will make a tremendous difference. Behind the green, a ladder makes bunkers and other hazards become clearly visible. I don't recommend standing on a golf cart, but finding a high spot on the course could improve your photo.

4. Try more than one lens and a polarizing filter to enhance a blue sky and dramatize clouds.

5. Check the sun's location. Shooting with the sun behind you will produce satisfactory, but less than dramatic, images. Sunlight shining at a ninety-degree angle to the fairway you're photographing will produce more attractive results.

6. Take a lot of photos and you're bound to get one that pleases.

— STEPHEN SZURLEJ

HEALTH AND FITNESS

307 How to stretch your muscles before you play

Place a towel between your head and the wall. Assume your address position, with your arms hanging down. Make a full shoulder turn on the backswing, keeping the left arm straight. Hold the position briefly. Swing through to the finish. Never let the towel drop. Let the right leg relax and the right knee bend inward on the follow-through. Hold briefly.   —JACK LALANNE

308 How to improve your swing while watching TV

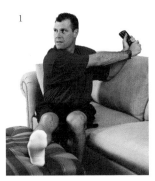

Spend three to four hours on the couch watching golf on TV last Sunday? Instead of vegging, here are three stretches you can do to stay limber for your next round:

1. To improve your backswing and follow-through: Hold the TV remote like a golf club and extend your right leg on an ottoman or stool. The left foot stays on the ground next to it. Make a full right-shoulder turn, so it's under your chin and your right arm is extended, as it would be when you follow through. Then repeat for the backswing by switching legs and turning in the other direction.

2. To stretch your glutes and improve hip mobility: Lie back on the couch, put your right foot on a coffee table or stool in front of you, and then put your left ankle on top of your right knee. Keep your back straight and extend your arms over your head. Try to elongate your spine as you feel the glutes muscle stretching. Then repeat with the other leg.

3. To stretch the hamstrings and shoulders: Extend your legs and stack your feet from toe to ankle. Then gradually lean forward. The goal is to touch your toes. Then switch the positions of the feet and repeat.

— RANDY MYERS

309 How to get into "golf shape"

If you want to start working out to ramp up your golf game, follow this advice:

1. Check with your physician before starting any fitness routine.

2. Ask whether your trainer has a background in golf. Be leery of trainers who offer "golf workouts" but don't play the game.

3. Avoid programs that take exercise genres and try to adapt them to golf. "Pilates for golfers" is Pilates for anyone.

4. Men generally gravitate toward strength training but need more flexibility. Women generally like flexibility programs but need to get stronger. Identify the area you need the most help with and focus on that.

5. If you're also taking golf lessons, make sure your fitness trainer knows. The trainer can tailor your workout to match your golf-swing practice. Often, there is a move or two in the golf swing that you might not be able to perform without some fitness training.

— RON KASPRISKE

310 How to loosen up in a hurry

You're late. You couldn't get out of that damn meeting. You're rushing to the course and there's no time to even tie your golf shoes. Follow this step-by-step method to loosen up:

1. Stretch in the car as you drive. With two hands on the wheel, flex your hands, roll your shoulders, stretch your neck, and shift your spine, all while breathing deeply. And keep your eyes on the road.

2. Get to the tee and grasp your sand wedge (the heaviest club) and 9-iron together. Make twenty long, slow swings.

3. Hold your sand wedge in your left arm. Put your feet together, lean as far as possible to your right, and do ten windmills, keeping your arm extended. Do ten more in the opposite direction. Repeat with your right arm, leaning left. This loosens your rotator cuff and the muscles running along your torso.

4. Ask to hit last, and take the extra time to make easy practice swings with your driver.

5. If you are riding in a cart, walk to your ball after your first tee shot. Your buddy will understand. You'll snag a few extra minutes to loosen up. Oh, yeah, and tie your shoes. —GUY YOCOM

helpful skills

203

311 How to treat golfer's elbow (tennis elbow too)

A common sore spot for golfers is the elbow. Pain and tenderness on the inner side of the joint, just above the funny bone, is known as golfer's elbow. If the pain is on the outer portion, it's known as tennis elbow and, believe it or not, it occurs about ten times as frequently for golfers as golfer's elbow (the tennis guys beat us to the term first).

To treat either, start with over-the-counter nonsteroidal painkillers. Take them before you play. After the round, ice will help reduce inflammation and prevent future problems. Standard forearm and wrist strengthening exercises can help.

Physical therapy and cortisone injections are options for severe cases, as is surgery. No one knows for sure what causes this condition. Overuse is the best theory. —RON KASPRISKE

THE LIGHTER SIDE

How to be in a relationship and play more golf

EDITOR'S NOTE: *This originally ran in* Golf Digest *as a serious article.*

Hankering to get in lots of golf this summer? Hoping you can plan a golf-full vacation? Here's how: Teach the little woman—friend, wife, gay companion, or just plain missus—to play golf! Don't be afraid that your wife will want to play along with you. She won't! For the average man is usually a superior golfer to the average woman, and knowing the ways of wives, you'll agree that they would not unwillingly place themselves in a position where their inferiority is so obvious!

Where is the golfing wife? Not at her husband's side—indeed, no! Blithely she ambles along with her feminine foursome, heedless of the passing hours and unconcerned as to the whereabouts of her mate. Though dimly aware that he might pause a bit too long at the nineteenth hole for the bracing cup that solves all problems, golfing and otherwise, she has no time to care!

The golfing wife is much more understanding. —PHIL GLANZER

312 How to treat your golf blisters

It probably wasn't such a good idea for your hands or feet to go back for that second extra-large bucket of range balls or to play forty-five holes in a day. But blisters are fairly common to golfers. Here are some tips for treating them:

• Drain the blister with a sterile needle. Pierce the edge, not the middle. Leave the layer of dead skin intact and dab antibiotic ointment on it.

• If the blister is on a finger or between two fingers, a simple bandage is sufficient to protect the area.

• If the blister is on the palm near the base of the fingers, protect the area with a product called "moleskin." You can cut moleskin to fit the area. Knuckle-shaped bandages will also do the trick but are less durable.

• If the blister is on the palm or heel of the hand, apply tincture of benzoin, an antiseptic liquid that adds a layer of protection over the raw skin. You'll also need padded bandages. Try a post-operation dressing such as OpSite, and cover thoroughly with a piece of moleskin.

—RON KASPRISKE

313 How to get through a golf trip with a bad back

If you wake up and your back is as stiff as a Retief Goosen press conference and you don't want to miss a tee time, here's some great advice from Ralph Simpson, a former PGA Tour certified physical therapist.

"Shortening the swing often allows you to continue playing before the back pain has completely subsided," Simpson says. "Also, toeing

out the lead foot slightly will decrease lower-back tension, especially if the lead hip is a bit restricted in range of motion. It will feel tight. When both hips are excessively tight—a problem called retroversion—both feet need to be slightly turned outward to reduce stress. These are only quick fixes, but should get you through the trip."

Two other musts: A hot shower before you play, to loosen up the muscles, and pain relievers to reduce inflammation. —RON KASPRISKE

314 How to know which painkiller to take

Ibuprofen (Advil): Good for muscle soreness in backs, knees, etc. Bad for your kidneys if the maximum daily dosage is taken for longer than three weeks.

Naproxen (Aleve): Good for joint pain and arthritis. Bad for golfers who don't use sunblock or wear sunglasses. It might increase the risk of sunburn and make the eyes sensitive to bright light.

Acetaminophen (Tylenol): Good for headaches, especially if you have an early tee time after a night on the town. Bad for your liver if you take more than 4,000 milligrams a day regularly.

Aspirin (Bayer): Good for dull pain. It also helps prevent heart disease and strokes. Bad for a sensitive stomach. Don't take the recommended daily dosage for more than a day or two.

—RON KASPRISKE

315 How to protect your skin from the sun when you play

Here's what you need to know about sunblock, according to Dr. Michael Kaminer of SkinCare Physicians. Kaminer is also a 6-handicapper.

• Gels and sprays are best. Sunblocks that are nongreasy, such as Coppertone Sport, are ideal for golfers. If you prefer lotions, consider Proderma, Blue Lizard, MenScience TiO2, or Sundurance MLT.

• Sunblock lasts only two hours. No matter what the sun-protection factor (SPF) is, you have to reapply every two hours. The amount golfers typically apply is about half what they need, so don't skimp.

• Focus on the ears, nose, scalp, and lips. These areas are either ignored when it comes to sun protection or highly susceptible to cancer. Use a lip balm with an SPF of fifteen or better. Spray sunblocks are OK for your hair or balding areas, but you should still wear a hat.

• SPF fifteen is the minimum. SPF one would protect you if you were standing outside on a sunny, summer day for ten minutes. You need fifteen times that to get through nine holes without burning your skin.

• Stop UVA and UVB rays. Use only sunblocks that protect against both types of ultraviolet rays. The fastest-acting sunblocks have titanium dioxide and/or zinc oxide, which are physical blockers. Chemical blockers work well but take up to thirty minutes to start working, so apply well before you go outdoors.

• Cloudy days do produce burns. Ultraviolet rays are always bouncing off you. So wear sunblock at all times. If you get burned, keep the area moisturized to avoid rashes, scabbing, and permanent scarring.

— RON KASPRISKE

316 How to avoid and deal with getting sunblock in your eyes

After two or three hours on the course, sunblock often starts to seep into your eyes. But is it really necessary to go temporarily blind from sunblock late in every round? Forget the claims of "sweatproof" sunblock. Instead, try these tricks to avoid bloodshot eyes.

• Wear a hat with a good sweatband. It will prevent most sunblock from sliding down past your forehead.

• Try dabbing your forehead (rather than rubbing it) with wipes, napkins, or a towel. — RON KASPRISKE

317 What to do when you encounter poison ivy

Poison ivy, found at many golf courses, can typically be identified by its three spade-shaped leaves (most often green, but also red). Sometimes greenish flowers and ivory-colored berries are near the stem.

If your skin touches poison ivy, don't scratch. Try to wash the area with soap within twenty minutes—even use water from a ball washer if you have to.

For an extreme case of poison ivy, see a doctor for a topical or systemic steroid preparation. Otherwise, treat with calamine lotion as soon as possible and repeat as needed. The rash can last as long as fourteen days. — RON KASPRISKE

318 What to eat for breakfast before you play

You're going to be on the golf course for four or five hours, and if you walk while carrying your bag it's possible to burn more than 2,000 calories. You need fuel for the journey, fuel that will keep you going for a long time. Considering a golfer's needs, here are the top choices for breakfast according to Dr. Diane Helsel, a nutrition expert at the University of Pittsburgh:

• Whole-grain bagel (plain or with jelly): It has carbohydrates for energy, fiber that lowers cholesterol, B vitamins for energy metabolism, and iron to get oxygen to the muscles.

• Oatmeal with raisins: It's high in carbs and provides soluble fiber. Raisins contain heart-healthy phytochemicals, plus iron, fiber, and potassium, which helps control blood pressure.

• Whole-grain cereal with skim milk and banana slices: A good source of fiber and fortified with vitamins and minerals. Milk has calcium, which helps prevent stress fractures, shin splints, and muscle cramps. Protein helps build and repair muscle, and the banana is rich in potassium, which is needed for muscle function.

• Low-fat yogurt with fresh berries: Yogurt has protein and calcium. Berries add ellagic acid (antioxidant with anticancer activity) and fiber.

• Sausage and biscuits with cream gravy. Just kidding.

— RON KASPRISKE

EDITOR'S NOTE: *We realize that many readers of this book are women, but since the overwhelming number of golfers in the U.S. are men (the National Golf Foundation estimates 75 to 80 percent), we decided to include a few gender-specific items. This was not done with the intention of offending women. In fact, we're hoping that the following advice will make the coexistence of men and women on the course more enjoyable.*

319 How to get your teenage daughter interested in golf

There's not much you can do to convince a fourteen-year-old of anything, especially if you're her parent. The only way you're going to get golf to compete with your daughter's social life is to ease off on the pressure and let her find the game on her own. Even if she feels a slight curiosity, she's probably repressing it just to go against your wishes. She's fourteen; that's her job. One approach is to try some reverse psychology. Stop talking to her about golf for a while. Let her know it's OK if she doesn't like the game but that you do. Then, on your next vacation (with none of her girlfriends around), take her to an LPGA tournament. Watching girls close to her own age hit booming drives in trendy outfits can do wonders for any teenager's perception of golf's cool factor. — STINA STERNBERG

How to fool your wife and sneak out to play golf

EDITOR'S NOTE: *This was written as a serious article in 1959.*

Spring is just around the corner. All across the land hopeful golfers are polishing up their irons, taking a few practice swings, and, most important, conjuring up a new crop of wool-puller-overs to get them past reluctant wives every afternoon there's a chance to play. Some husbands are more ingenious than others in this business of hoodwinking the better half into getting in that extra game of golf. As a public service to the more timid golfers, we offer the following surefire suggestions:

1. "I was in to see Doc Jones yesterday. Been feeling a twinge of the old back trouble lately. He says I should get more exercise in the sun." (Doc Jones is actually a veterinarian and also a member of your foursome.)

2. "There's a big business deal we've been working on at the office all week. Some fellows from an out-of-town firm have been working with us, and they thought we might clear away some of the cobwebs by taking a break out at the club this afternoon." (Truth is you've come across a couple of certified pigeons, and the big deal involves a side bet you're pretty sure you can win hands down.)

3. "You know something, honey—it's really cheaper to play a round with the boys than stay home. I usually pick up some lunch money this way, and today I think I can win enough to take you out to that new supper club."

4. "I've had a strange feeling lately that this may be the last summer I'll be able to enjoy the game. I'm not getting any younger, you know."

5. "I was going to fix that broken place in the fence this afternoon, but Bob just called and said his brother-in-law was visiting and wants to know if I can join them. Bob said he knew what a good

helpful skills

sport you were." (Under no circumstances would she admit to not being a good sport.)

6. "Why don't you play a few holes with me this afternoon?" (You know you're safe in asking because this is the day for the monthly meeting of her Stitch and Chatter Club. Chances are she'll tell you to run along and find someone else to play with.)

7. "I'm playing golf this afternoon, and if you don't like it, you know what to do." (I knew a fellow who tried this and found himself sailing through the air. His bride had neglected to tell him she was a former judo instructor.) —H. N. FERGUSON

320 How to play quickly with a girlfriend or wife

There's a fine line between being rude and maintaining pace of play. Women like to be taken seriously on the course. If you act as if it's a waste of time for your wife to execute any putt less than five feet, you're telling her she's a lousy player and her score doesn't matter. Even worse is when a guy sticks out a foot to stop a woman's chip from going across the green. Where do you find *that* in *The Rules of Golf*? Instead, help her read the putt, and try to make sure you both keep a healthy pace between shots. —STINA STERNBERG

321   How to cope with an angry partner

When your girlfriend or wife plays poorly, let her get frustrated without interfering. You might think you're helping by pointing out what's wrong, but you're only making her more upset. I'll let you in on a secret: women come with a built-in notion that men can and should read our minds. My advice to guys in these situations is to resist the urge to fix everything. Instead, keep your mouth shut.

—STINA STERNBERG

322   How to play a competitive match against your wife

If you believe you have to fold a match to keep your girlfriend or wife in a good mood, I'm afraid you have bigger problems than I can help you with. Letting her win might seem like an easy way to keep her happy, but it will only lead to more trouble. You have to be a good actor to pull off a believable fold, and you'll always know that you threw the match, which also means she'll likely sense it. In the long run, she'll resent you more for that than for beating her fair and square. The balance of your relationship will shift. If your significant other is the type of person who can't stand losing to her boyfriend, then don't play matches against her. Pair up as a team and take on other couples instead. Then you'll be equals.   —STINA STERNBERG

323 How to get and keep your girlfriend or wife interested in golf

Take your girlfriend or wife to the range and patiently let her learn the game. In fact, don't go near a course until she understands the basics of the swing and has felt that rush of making solid contact at least a few dozen times. Keep it fun, and don't overwhelm her with too much information. If you sense she likes it, let a teaching pro take over and stay out of the instruction. Once she starts to hit the ball with some success, get her fitted for clubs, buy a few, and go play nine. A cool pair of golf shoes can help seal the deal: the average *Golf for Women* magazine reader owns seven pairs. One more thing: resist giving her a full-on golf lesson on the course.

—STINA STERNBERG

Equipment

Golf equipment poses a real dilemma for most amateur players. While it's likely that buying a top-of-the-line driver or set of irons will help their games, investing hundreds to thousands of dollars on things that are used only ten to twenty times a year might seem frivolous.

However, advances in club and ball manufacturing have been so rapid and effective in recent years that if you're using a driver or golf ball that's more than a few years old, you're at a real disadvantage against a golfer who has the latest stuff. And it's not just a matter of walking into the local sporting goods store or logging on to eBay and buying the first TaylorMade, Titleist, or Callaway club you see. Golfers who are serious about getting better are getting custom-fit for their clubs. They are also selecting golf balls based on their swing speed and typical shot shape.

So if you're interested in buying new equipment, this chapter is for you. Led by advice from *Golf Digest* senior equipment editor Mike Stachura, the following tips should help you enjoy the game more, improve your chances of lowering your scores, and keep you from wasting money on things you don't want or need.

324 What do all these equipment terms really mean?

EDITOR'S NOTE: *Golf equipment seemingly has its own language. Rather than include these in the general glossary (page 231), we decided, for convenience, to list them and their definitions here.*

BOUNCE: The degree to which the sole of a club angles up and away from the ground plane when the club is in a square setup position. In general, the more bounce, the better the club is for soft sand and high, lush grass; less bounce is better for firm sand and firm turf.

BULGE: The face curvature from heel to toe that corrects spin on mishits.

CAMBER: The radius measurement of the sole from front to back or heel to toe.

CENTER OF GRAVITY (CG): A theoretical point that defines the average location of weight in a clubhead and the internal point about which an object rotates. A low CG helps to launch the ball higher. A club's CG isn't always found at its geometric center.

CHAMFER: A beveled or rounded edge connecting two surfaces.

COEFFICIENT OF RESTITUTION (COR): Used by manufacturers to refer to the springlike effect of a flexing clubface. The USGA COR limit of 0.83 refers to the efficiency of energy transfer between two colliding bodies (clubhead and ball). The way a thin titanium clubface flexes can reduce the way the ball deforms at impact, therefore decreasing the loss of energy transfer to the ball.

LEADING EDGE: The forward edge of the sole, opposite the trailing edge.

MOMENT OF INERTIA (MOI): The measure of a club's resistance to twisting on off-center hits (sometimes called forgiveness).

RELIEF: The angling, or the curve up and back, of the sole to reduce turf contact.

SKIRT: The perimeter of a clubhead between the sole and the crown.

—MAX ADLER

equipment

325 What you should know before buying golf clubs

- Before you add a lob wedge to your bag, practice with it—a lot.
- Most golfers don't have enough bounce on their sand wedge.
- Dump your 3-iron and 4-iron, and replace them with hybrids.
- Out of four-inch rough, grooves play no part in performance.
- A face-balanced, mallet-style putter forgives your sins on the green.
- A gap wedge is essential for success around the greens.
- If you want to carry two drivers, they should have different lofts, not hook- or slice-correcting features.
- Unsure whether you should use a stiff or regular shaft? Go for the regular first.
- With a clubhead speed of eighty to ninety m.p.h., launch the ball at fourteen degrees with a spin rate of 3,000-plus r.p.m. for maximum distance.
- Try to hit the ball a little above the sweet spot on your driver to take advantage of the vertical gear effect (less spin, higher launch).
- A ten-m.p.h. headwind will shorten your drive 30 percent more than a ten-m.p.h. tailwind will help.
- A 150-yard shot to a green elevated ten degrees will play approximately 175 yards, a two-club difference. —FRANK THOMAS

326 How to get a perfect custom fit

Not getting custom fit for clubs is like buying underwear without checking the size first. Most larger retailers, such as Golfsmith, Golf Galaxy, and Golf Headquarters, provide full-service fitters at their shops.

Here's what to look for:

• Make sure there is a launch monitor and qualified operator. A good selection of shaft and loft options is a must.

• Be prepared to pay a fee. Fitting sessions range from no charge to $150 per club and run a half-hour to three hours.

• Before committing yourself to the recommendations from an indoor fitting session, see if you can demo some options outdoors. Ball flight is the ultimate confirmation. —MIKE STACHURA

THE LIGHTER SIDE

How to treat a misbehaving driver

My driver has been misbehaving, so I had to give it a time-out. I moved it to the back of the bag and pulled the headcover down tight. Some guys will abuse a driver that has launched a ball into an adjacent county, but believe me, the short-fuse approach doesn't work with golf clubs any better than it does with children. You can't straighten a slice with violence and fear. Rather than screaming at my equipment when it lets me down, I try to praise it when it does something right. Most golfers will curse a shank yet stand smugly silent when their 7-iron stripes a ball straight at the pin. How would you like it if your boss took credit for all your best efforts and never spoke to you except to pick on your mistakes? Even when a shot of mine goes wrong, I try to find something encouraging to say: "Wasn't that a little draw I noticed just before you bounced into the parking lot?" "I don't believe you've ever driven it farther into the pond." —DAVID OWEN

327 How to use a launch monitor

A launch monitor is a portable computer used to record the speed and path of your swings and how they affect your ball flight. Using a launch monitor yields important information about your swing. Here's how to do it:

• Spend at least an hour on it to get usable data. Average strikes, not your best hits, are what really matter.

• Pay attention to your ball speed. Every one-mile-per-hour of increased ball speed equates to two and a half yards, so do anything you can to increase ball speed.

• If you swing a driver less than 100 miles per hour, launch angle is crucial. For those who swing faster, spin plays a great role. If you can average less than 200 revolutions per minute per degree of launch (twelve degrees and 2,400 r.p.m., for example), you're on the right track.

• Use the ball you prefer to play. Do not use range balls. Your numbers will be more accurate. —MIKE STACHURA

328 How to buy a driver that doesn't slice

Some things can't be fixed. If your swing includes a severe outside-to-in downswing, nothing short of reconstructive surgery and a lobotomy will fix your slice. For others, there are a few key driver tweaks that could help rein in those wild tee shots. An offset clubhead and a more flexible shaft are two options. An increase in loft also reduces sidespin. But the biggest slice fighters are length and weight. A shorter (forty-four inches long) and heavier (increase the weight by fifteen to twenty grams) shaft will improve the clubhead's resistance to twisting on off-center hits. A club with a closed clubface can also help. —MIKE STACHURA

329 How to determine the correct loft in a driver

In 2003, *Golf Digest* tested golfers with average swing speeds and concluded they needed more loft than they thought they needed in their drivers. In 2008, we found similar results, but we also found that it's awfully easy to overdose on loft. More loft is good, but too much seems to be much worse than too little.

Our testing featured players with swing speeds either at seventy-five or at ninety-five miles per hour using drivers with lofts from nine to sixteen degrees. The slower swinger benefited almost equally from the twelve- and fourteen-degree drivers, which carried about fifteen yards farther than the nine-degree driver. The nine-degree driver rolled an average of thirty-two yards but went only one yard less than the sixteen-degree driver for seventy-five-m.p.h. swingers and five yards more for the ninety-five-m.p.h. swingers.

So the best results came with a twelve-degree driver for both groups.

— MIKE STACHURA

330 How to determine which iron a hybrid should replace

When replacing irons with hybrids, do not replace a twenty-one-degree 3-iron with a twenty-one-degree hybrid. The reason? The mass of a hybrid will produce a shot that flies farther. Instead, you should replace irons with hybrids of slightly higher lofts. That 3-iron should be replaced with a twenty-three-degree hybrid, for example. You will maintain the same distance you had with the iron, and also hit the ball at a higher trajectory, making it easier to stop the ball on the green.

— RON KASPRISKE

equipment

331 How many wedges should you carry?

The average amateur struggles with two things when it comes to wedge play:

1. Hitting shots that require less than a full swing.

2. Hitting wedge shots high enough and with enough spin to stop the ball on the putting surface.

With this pair of problems in mind, we think it makes sense to carry four wedges. Rather than simply going out and buying a pitching wedge, gap wedge, sand wedge, and lob wedge, tell the retailer you want wedges with no more than five degrees' difference in loft from one club to the next. For example, if the pitching wedge has forty-seven degrees of loft, the gap wedge should have fifty-one or fifty-two degrees, and if you then buy a fifty-two-degree gap wedge, the sand wedge should be fifty-six or fifty-seven degrees, and so on.

Also, make sure one of the wedges (probably the lob wedge) has less bounce than the others. While you need bounce in the sand, it's good to carry a wedge that can chip or pitch the ball high off of tight lies. A lot of bounce hinders your chances of doing that. Less bounce also helps with shots out of wet sand. —RON KASPRISKE

332 What to remember before buying a putter

You're about to buy a putter, and you've just noticed there are a few hundred varieties on the market. Before your head explodes, follow these steps and you'll get the one you want:

1. Get fitted. The length of the putter's shaft is important. Unless it's a long or belly putter, most experts recommend that the shaft length be no longer than the height at which the arms can hang freely and grip the club.

2. Roll putts with both mallet-headed putters and blades. Decide which looks the best and putts the best.

3. Try the belly and the long putters too. Some people love them; others hate them. But if either style works for you, use it.

4. Once you have a model in mind, have your alignment checked and the putter adjusted to it. Lasers can be used to adjust a putter's head if you tend to aim left or right of your target because of being dominant in one eye. —RON KASPRISKE

333 Should you buy steel or graphite shafts?

The good news is that quality control is so good nowadays that there aren't many bad shafts, but there are hundreds of varieties. So here's what you need to know before buying steel or graphite shafts.

There has been a lot of experimentation with materials for shafts besides steel. From 1966 to 1974, before I joined the USGA, I worked as chief design engineer for the Shakespeare sporting goods company, where I developed new techniques to make golf shafts, first using fiberglass and then with graphite fibers supplied by Union Carbide. The technique was to wrap epoxy-impregnated bundles of fibers onto a thin steel rod. This, in turn, was wrapped with a cellophane sheath and then hung in an oven to cure. After the epoxy set, the steel rod (or mandrel) was withdrawn, leaving a hollow shaft made of graphite fibers and epoxy.

The major benefit of graphite is that it's much lighter than steel—a typical graphite shaft weighs slightly more than two ounces, about half the weight of a steel shaft. That means it may be possible to swing the club a little faster with the same energy, and thus one may be able to gain about five yards of distance on average. There are other claims for graphite—that it allows you to "feel" the clubhead more, for example, or that it is easier on your joints, reducing the risk of golfer's elbow—which may or may not be true. The downside is that a quality graphite shaft is still more expensive than steel.

Shaft makers have also experimented with mixing other materials—such as Kevlar, glass, steel, or boron fibers—with graphite. Now there are shafts in which one section is made of steel and another of graphite, such as the new BiMatrx shafts from True Temper and the GT iron shafts from Adams Golf.

Of course, the most important aspect of any shaft is not the material it's made from but how it performs—for you. Make sure a shaft has the right flex. A broomstick is too stiff; a fishing rod is too whippy. As with the hickory shafts of old, only trial and error will allow you to find the shaft that feels right. — FRANK THOMAS

334 How to tell if your clubs are fakes

Many clubs on the market today are counterfeit. Most of the fakes are made in China and, in some instances, are assembled in the same factory as the real clubs they are trying to copy.

To avoid buying a fake or to see if the club you are playing is an impostor, follow these steps:

1. Buy from a reputable dealer. Most counterfeit clubs are offered only online and usually for considerably less than the real manufacturer's suggested retail price.

2. Check for a serial number and call the club manufacturer to verify that it's legit.

3. Look for imperfections to the markings on the club against the real thing. Many of the labels and colors can be slightly different. They should be easy to spot.

4. If it's a driver or fairway wood, tap the head with a coin. If it makes a ping sound, it's probably not made with legit materials.

335 How to understand the difference between golf balls

There are four primary kinds of golf balls: the two-piece distance ball, the two-piece low-compression ball, the multilayer ball with an ionomer cover (such as Surlyn), and the multilayer ball with a polyurethane cover (most tour balls). These balls behave differently for different shots, but just how different are they on full swings? To test, we had a double-digit handicapper with a swing speed of

equipment

95 miles per hour (about the average) and a scratch player with a swing speed of 105 miles per hour hit these balls with a driver and a 9-iron.

When we distilled the averages of both players, the range was surprisingly tight among the four balls. The difference between the highest and the lowest bar was seven yards in driver carry distance, 900 revolutions per minute in driver spin, and five yards in 9-iron height. Launch monitors sometimes tell only part of the story. Though the two-piece distance ball flew the highest, it also tended to roll the farthest from its pitch mark once it hit the green.

—MAX ADLER

336 What about cavity-back irons or forged irons?

If you're not sure whether to buy a cavity-back or forged set of irons, remember this: simply put, golfers looking for a clubhead that propels the ball reasonably well even if they don't make center-face contact will want a cavity-back iron. Cavity back means the weight of the clubhead is distributed around the edges, allowing for more forgiveness on off-center hits. High-handicap players benefit the most from these clubs. Forged irons have most of their clubhead mass centered. So better players, who are looking to shape shots and maximize their distance with irons, are better off with forged clubs.

—RON KASPRISKE

337 How to pick the right ball

The fastest route to improving your game might be as simple as changing your ball. In fact, John Calabria, *Golf Digest's* technical adviser, says the right ball for an average player might solve the problem of underclubbing, as it will give the player ten extra yards. Switching to a two-piece ball could give the average player more distance with the irons.

Also, your ball should fit your course. Fast, firm conditions call for a multilayer, urethane-covered ball—the ones the tour pros use. On the other hand, if your venue is lush, slow, or wet, a two-piece performance ball is a smarter choice. —MIKE STACHURA

338 What you need to know about used golf balls

If you're considering buying used golf balls, defective balls from manufacturers (known as x-outs), or a golf ball reclaimed from water, consider this information: A ball that is two years old or older loses about 2 to 3 percent of its distance potential. An x-out ball is not only likely to be nonconforming (check the USGA's list at usga.org); it also has a minor defect that would keep it from performing as well as a good ball from the same manufacturer. And a ball that was submerged in water for a week flies six yards shorter than a regular golf ball. —RON KASPRISKE

339 What is the importance of clubhead speed?

If you're interested in hitting the ball farther, then you're interested in swinging the club faster. Why? Every mile per hour you swing a club equals two and a half yards of carry for a golf ball. So consider buying lighter clubs to increase your swing speed. —MAX ADLER

340 What is moment of inertia, and why should I care?

MOI, which means "moment of inertia," is a term you've probably heard a lot. Technically, this is a "measure of resistance to angular acceleration," which means how rapidly a clubhead will twist during impact when a golfer misses the sweet spot. It relates to all clubs, including putters.

High MOI, a good thing for amateurs, is achieved by moving weight far away from the center of gravity. Distributing weight in this manner gives optimum forgiveness on all mishits, both high and low as well as heel and toe. Even putters with high MOI will be better balanced and tend to stay steadier through impact. Think of MOI as MOF (measure of forgiveness). —FRANK THOMAS

341 How to get your golf equipment ready for golf season

You've been waiting all winter for this shining moment when you can get your equipment out of the garage and back into your recreation rotation. Here are a handful of things to do before you start to use it again:

• Clean your clubs with warm water and a stiff nylon brush (not wire). You wouldn't use Brillo on your car, would you?

• Wash your grips with warm water too. Or, better yet, get new grips.

• Machine-wash your towel—twice. It has enough mold on it to make cheese.

• Inspect your bag carefully for candy bars, bananas, chewing tobacco. If you find any, you might want to call a local hazmat crew to have them removed.

• Replace the insoles in your shoes or, for the sake of your friends and family, remove them, wash them, and sprinkle them with foot powder before replacing them.

• Apply leather conditioner (cream) to your shoes. Do not wax them. Replace the spikes and laces.

• That shriveled-up black thing used to be a glove. Get a new one—and balls and long tees.   —MARTY HACKEL

342 How to polish your golf shoes

Don't. The first thing you should do is clean, not polish, your shoes. A damp cloth with a little soapy water should do the trick, or you can take care of them with a clean shoe-polish applicator brush. After cleaning, wipe them dry with a soft cloth (an old towel is perfect). Let 'em dry.

Most shoes today have uppers that are waterproof. Apply cream conditioner to these periodically. Stay away from wax, which will prevent them from breathing. Don't use that white liquid polish (only a shoe pro knows how to apply it).   —MARTY HACKEL

343 How to pick the right cleats

If you really take your traction seriously, consider the type of turf on which you're playing and rotate your cleats accordingly. On hardpan, your shoe needs to pierce the earth. On lush grass, your shoe needs to tangle with the blades of grass. Therefore, for hardpan conditions, use a cleat made of rigid plastic with fewer but sharper prongs. On a lush course, with healthy rough, use a softer, pliable cleat with more prongs.

A set of cleats typically lasts fifteen rounds, though certain new models have wear indicators.   —MIKE STACHURA

Glossary

ARC: The path a clubhead travels on.

ADDRESS: The posture a golfer takes right before he or she hits the ball. Note: According to *The Rules of Golf,* you have not addressed a ball until you have taken your stance and grounded your club (except in a hazard).

BACK/REAR FOOT: The foot that is farther away from the target.

BACK UP: When backspin makes a ball roll toward you at the end of a shot.

BOUNCE: The flange on the bottom of the club.

BUTT OF THE CLUB: The top of the grip end of the club.

CHECK: When a ball stops because of backspin.

CHIPPING: A low-trajectory short shot played anywhere from just off the green to roughly fifty yards away, but typically played around the green.

CLOSED OR HOODED FACE: When the clubface is pointing left of the target at address or impact (for right-handed players).

CLOSED STANCE: When your shoulders and body are aligned right of the target (for right-handed players).

CLUB-LENGTH: A unit of measurement (typically determined using the length of the driver) to determine where to drop a ball.

DIAL IN: To accurately judge the distance a club can hit a ball.

EXTENSION: Keeping the arms extended during the swing.

FADING: For right-handed players, a shot that gradually curves left to right.

FEATHERING: A shot that appears to move and land gently.

FLYER LIE: When the back of the ball is covered by grass, this produces a shot that has less backspin and tends to fly farther than normal.

FOLLOW-THROUGH: The portion of the golf swing after the ball is struck until the club and body stop moving.

FINISH: The end of the golf swing.

FORECADDIE: A type of caddie that doesn't carry your clubs (if you are riding in a golf cart) but stays ahead of your group and marks where your ball lands, among other duties.

FRIED EGG: A ball that rests in a deep-impact crater in the sand. The combination of ball and crater creates a yolk-and-egg-white look.

FRONT FOOT: The foot that is closer to the target.

GRIP DOWN (ALSO KNOWN AS CHOKING DOWN): Gripping the club slightly closer to the clubhead than normal.

GROUND UNDER REPAIR: Any area designated by the course you are playing as unfit for use. If your ball is in the designated area, you get relief without penalty.

HANDICAP: A mathematical formula used to assign a player a number based on the ten best scores of his or her last twenty rounds in order to allow that player to compete on relatively equal ground with a player who has a different skill level.

HANDS AHEAD: When your club is in a position so your hands are closer to the target than the clubhead.

HARDPAN: Any grassless surface of the course that is firm.

HAZARD: Any bunker or water hazard. You are not allowed to ground your club at address in a hazard (one-stroke penalty).

HINGING OR COCKING THE WRISTS: To allow your wrists to bend. For a right-handed player, the move is typically to allow the right wrist to cup and the left wrist to bow.

HOOK: A shot that curves severely right to left (for right-handed players).

HOT: A shot that has little backspin, flies low, and rolls a great distance before stopping.

LEADING EDGE: The bottom edge of the clubface.

LOB OR FLOP SHOT: A short pitch with an extremely high trajectory.

LOCAL RULE: Any rule designated by the golf course that is not a part of the normal rules and can be applied only in the specific situation of that course.

LOOSE IMPEDIMENTS: Natural objects that are not fixed, growing, solidly embedded, or adhering to the ball.

MULLIGAN: A do-over. Practiced worldwide but against the rules.

OPEN CLUBFACE: When the face is pointing right of the target (for right-handed players).

OPEN STANCE: When your shoulders and body are aligned left of your target (for right-handed players).

OUT-TO-IN/IN-TO-OUT SWINGS: The path the club takes in relation to the target line. Out-to-in means the club is outside the target line during the downswing and inside during the follow-through. The reverse is true for in-to-out swings.

OUTSIDE AGENCY: Anything that is not a part of your match or, in stroke play, not part of the competitor's side and includes a referee, a marker, an observer, and a forecaddie.

PINCH: When the clubhead perfectly makes contact with the ball at the point where the ball touches the ground.

PITCHING: A high-trajectory short shot that is typically played from ten to sixty years from the green.

PLAY THE BALL BACK/FORWARD: The position of the ball at address. A ball back would be closer to the back foot (right foot for right-handed players).

PLAY THROUGH: Allowing a faster group on a course to move ahead of the group in front of them.

PRESS: A gambling term that means to start a new bet, usually for the same amount as the current bet, and is only for a predetermined amount of holes starting at that point. For example, if there are three holes left in a match, the player who is losing can start a new bet for the remaining three holes.

PULL: A ball that flies on a straight path left of the target (for right-handed players).

PUNCHOUT: A low, running, easy-to-control shot used to get out of trouble and back onto the fairway.

PUSH OR BLOCK: A ball that flies on a straight path right of the target (for right-handed players).

RELEASE: Allowing the forearms to rotate counterclockwise and the clubface to close as a player swings through the ball.

SHALLOW: A golf swing that approaches the ball on an angle more horizontal than normal.

SHORT-SIDED: When the pin is closely tucked toward the edge of the green you are closest to.

SLICE: A ball that severely curves in a left-to-right path (for right-handed players).

SPINE TILT: At address, the angle of the spine in relation to the ground.

SQUARE: When the clubface is exactly perpendicular to something—for example, the target line.

STEEP: A golf swing that approaches the ball on an angle more vertical than normal.

STRONG GRIP: A position of the hands on the club where the thumbs favor the right side (for right-handed players).

SWING PLANE: The angle that the shaft and the ground create when a golfer addresses the ball and then swings the club.

SWING PATH: The path the clubhead travels from address to finish.

TOE: The edge of the clubface farthest away from the shaft.

TOP OF THE SWING: The point of the golf swing where the backswing ends and the downswing is about to begin.

WAGGLE: To rapidly sway the club back and forth, usually with the wrists, before a player hits a shot in an effort to reduce tension and make the start of the golf swing more dynamic.

WEAK GRIP: A position of the hands on the club where the thumbs favor the left side (for right-handed players).

WINTER RULES: A phrase used by golfers giving them permission to improve their lie on wet, muddy, winter days. There is no such rule allowing this. However, a course can enact a local rule of lift, clean, and place if the conditions warrant.

Acknowledgments

I'd like to thank several people for their contributions to this book: Jerry Tarde, Bob Carney, Byrtue Johnson, Lisa Sweet, Marne Mayer, Tara Fucale, Jeanmarie Ferullo, and Mark Wilson.

And a very special thanks goes to photographers J.D. Cuban, Dom Furore, Stephen Szurlej, and Jim Herity. Their great work is displayed throughout these pages.

Index of Contributors

Subject Index